POSITION OF THE DAY

REVISED AND UPDATED

POSITION OF THE DAY

SEX EVERY DAY IN EVERY WAY

★ REVISED AND UPDATED ★

FROM NERVE.COM

CHRONICLE BOOKS
SAN FRANCISCO

Library of Congress Cataloging-in-Publication Data available.
ISBN: 978-1-7972-3722-0

Manufactured in India.

MIX
Paper | Supporting responsible forestry
FSC www.fsc.org FSC™ C043100

Design by Venus D'Amore. Typesetting by Frank Brayton.

10 9 8 7 6 5 4 3 2 1

Chronicle Books LLC
680 Second Street
San Francisco, California 94107
www.chroniclebooks.com

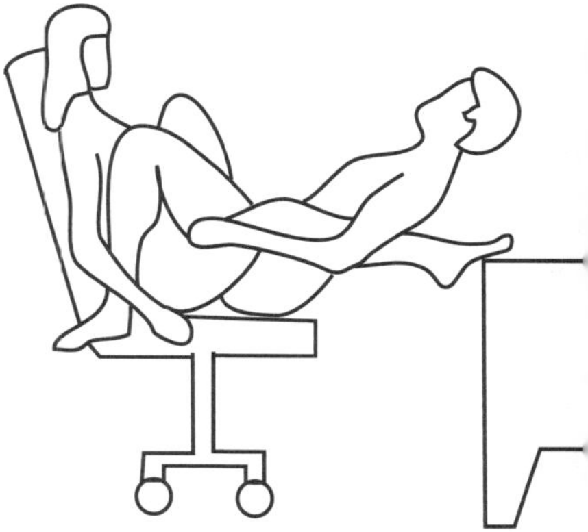

INTRODUCTION

When we first started publishing the Position of the Day on *Nerve.com*, it never occurred to us that couples would actually try these positions—or that this would turn into a bestselling series. Yet, here we are! This newly revised edition features all the classics, plus reimagined positions and essential updates—all with the end goal of making sex fun and inclusive for everyone.

Originally, we were more interested in coming up with clever names than dishing practical sex advice. Take "The Double-Doggy," for example (June 4)—even if you did happen to own a rocking chair, you'd have to be a professional acrobat to attempt intercourse in this position. Or so we thought.

But our resourceful readers had other ideas, and they started regaling us with tales of their attempts of "Climbing Mount Pleasant" (June 16; fortunately, none of them sent pictures). Some wanted us to rate positions for difficulty; others got offended when we included positions that were obviously impossible, like "The Three O'Clock" (December 14), and still others wondered how they were expected to get by on only one new position a day.

Perhaps it was the silly nicknames that made the positions—and actually bringing them into play—seem more like a game than work. Couples are often loath to consult sex manuals for "inspiration" because it's like admitting that there's something wrong, that something needs to be fixed, that the so-called spark is gone. But it's nothing to be ashamed of—we all become creatures of habit at some point. Hey, orgasms are good things, and sometimes you just want to take the shortest route to your happy place. But even "The Happy Landing" (June 25) can get boring if that's all you do. And half the fun of an orgasm is the journey there. How's that for "inspiration"?

But this isn't a textbook sex manual, damn it, and we don't have any interest in fixing sex. We're not telling you the way sex should be; we're just providing the raw material for your own interpretation. Plus, you don't have to beat yourself up if you can't master all these positions because a third of them are impossible anyway. (Or a quarter if you stretch first.)

Think of this book as a preemptive strike—why wait 'til you're in the dreaded rut and actually need one of those sex manuals to swing from the rafters and yell, "I Can See My House from Here!" (February 27). The moment you think you know all there is to know about sex is the moment your sex life is over. The first step is admitting you need help. The second step is admitting you need this book. The third step is buying it.

— The *Nerve* staff

THE POSITIONS

>

january.) **01**

HAPPY NEW YEAR

january.) **02**

THE RECLINER

january.)

03

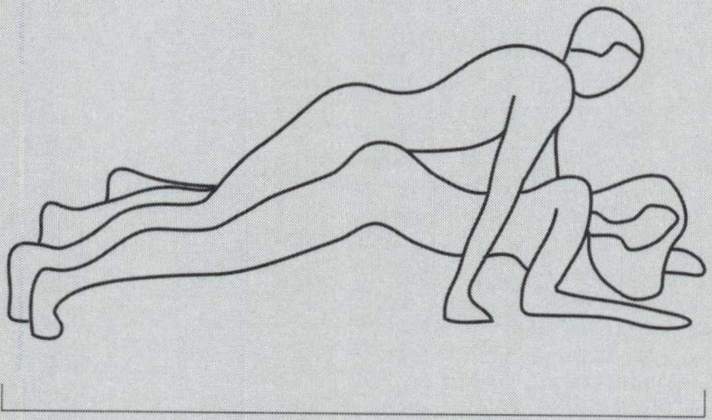

THE DROP AND GIVE ME 20

january.) 04

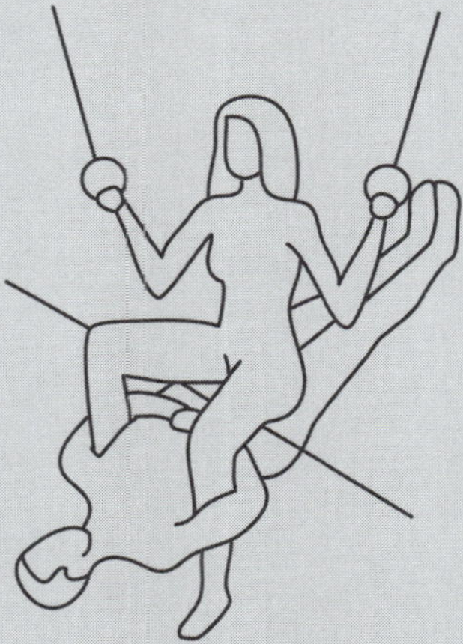

THE HOME GYM

january.)

05

HIP HIP HOORAY

january.) 06

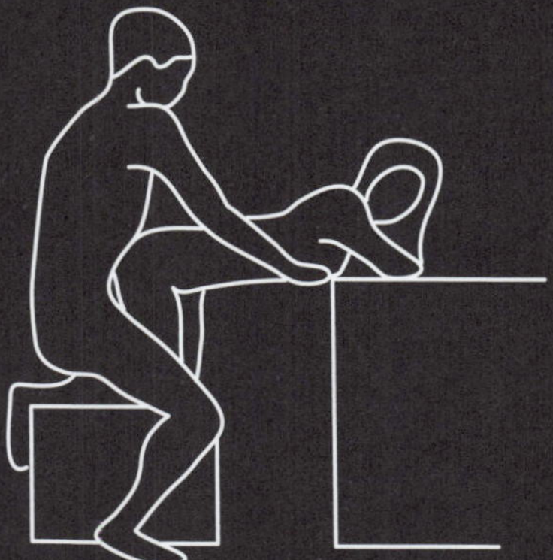

NOTHING'S OFF THE TABLE

january.)

07

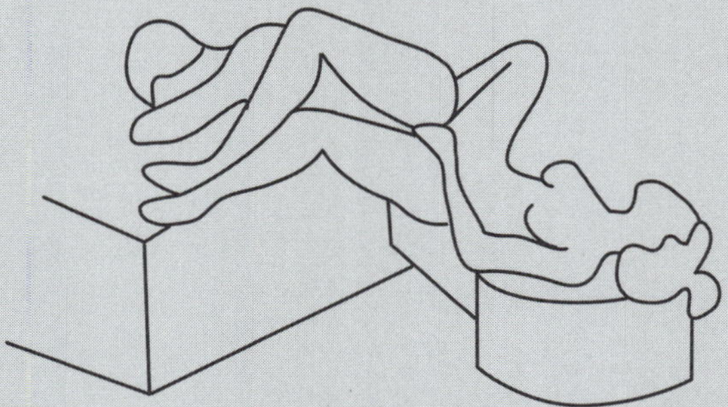

WHOSE LEG IS IT ANYWAY?

january.)

08

WALK THE PLANK

january.) **09**

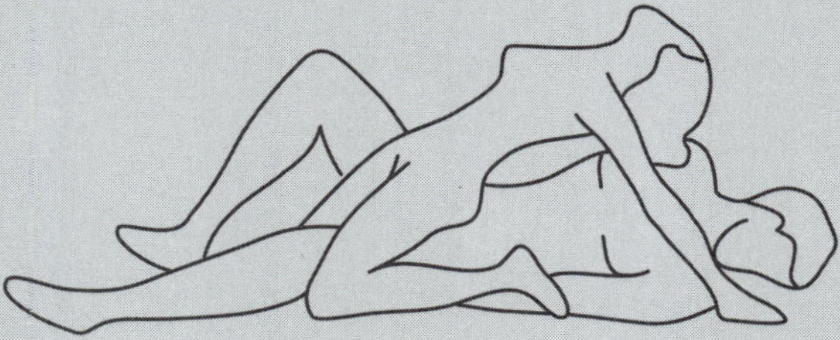

THE CHRYSALIS

THE DOUBLE HELIX

january.)

11

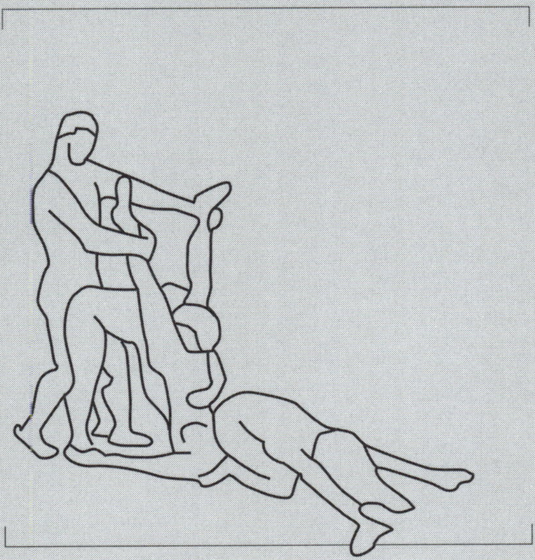

THE WELL-OILED MACHINE

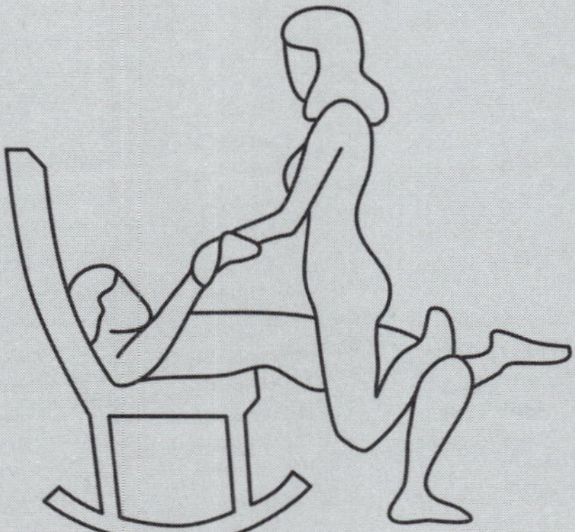

THE BETTY ROCKER

january.) **13**

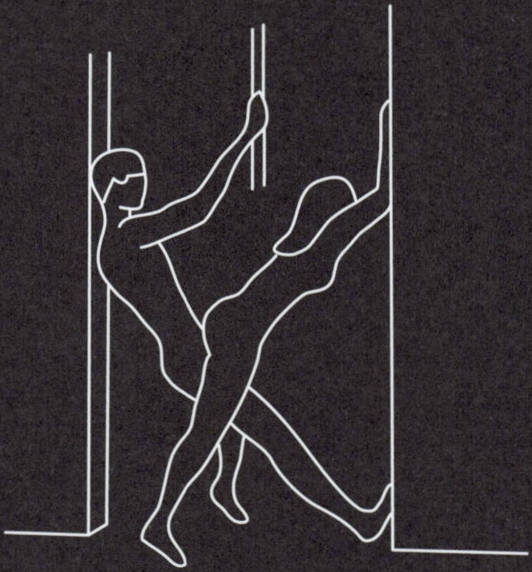

YOU RANG?

THE SEESAW

january.)

15

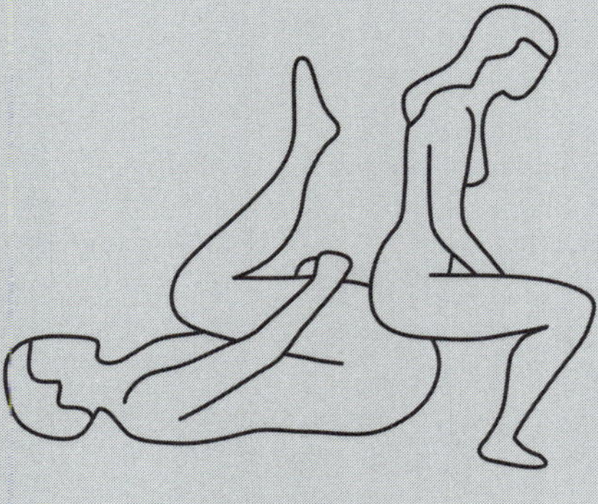

GOING CAMPING

january.) **16**

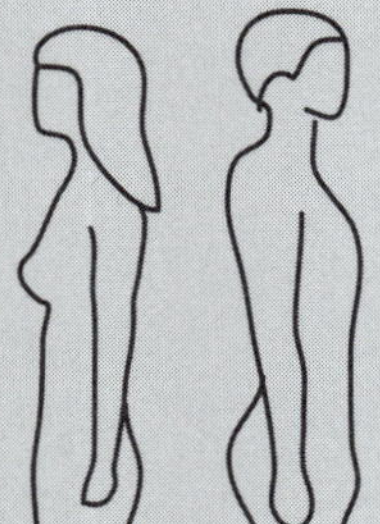

THE HEADACHE

january.)

17

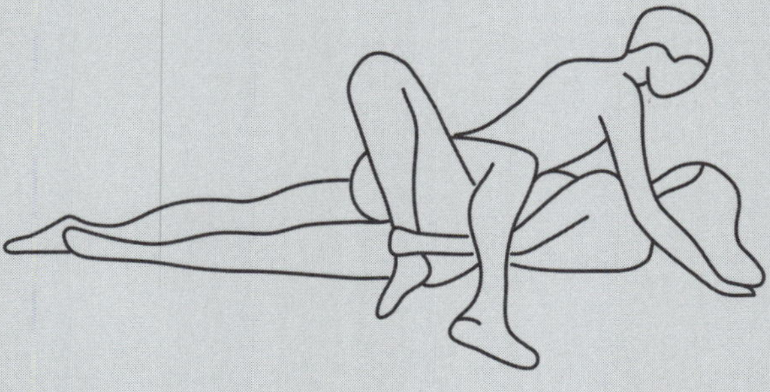

THE HAMSTRING SANDWICH

january.)

18

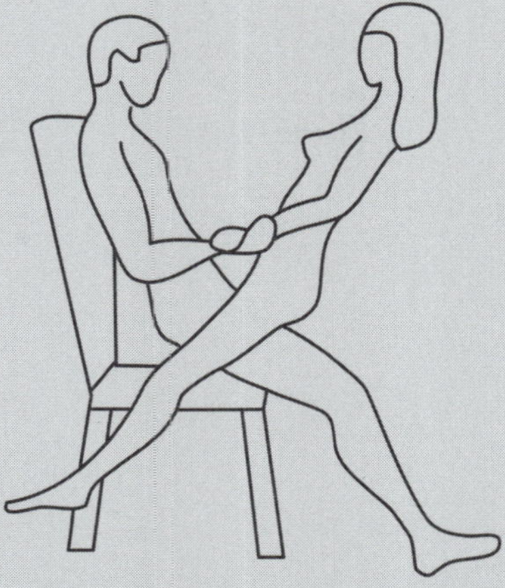

THE TEETER-TOTTER

january.) 19

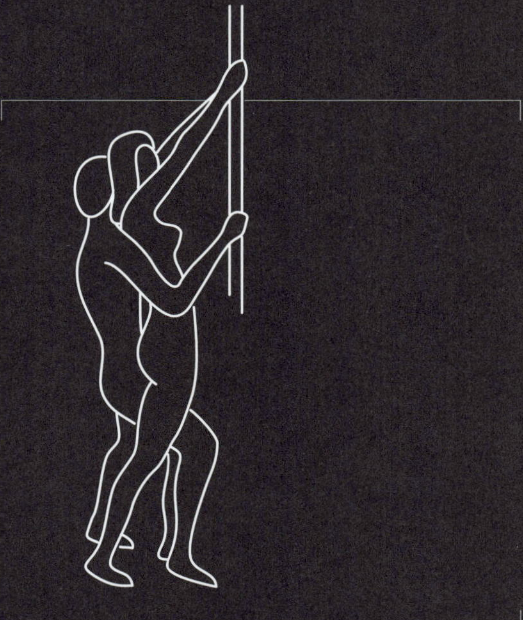

THE HOLD TIGHT

january.)

20

THE THIGH HIGH

january.)

21

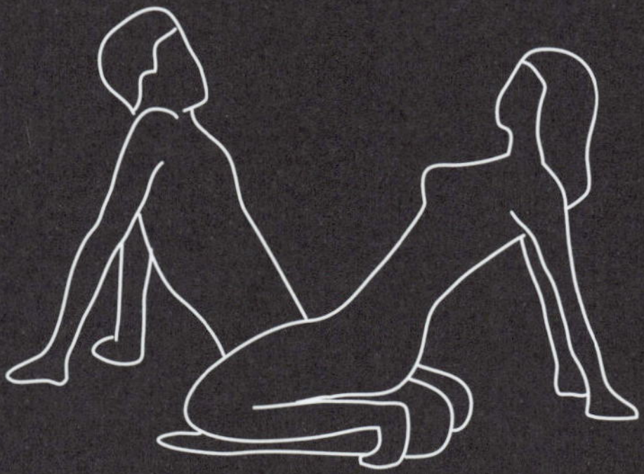

THE MAKE ENDS MEET

january.)

22

THE HOME STRETCH

january.)

23

PUT YOUR BACK INTO IT

january.)

24

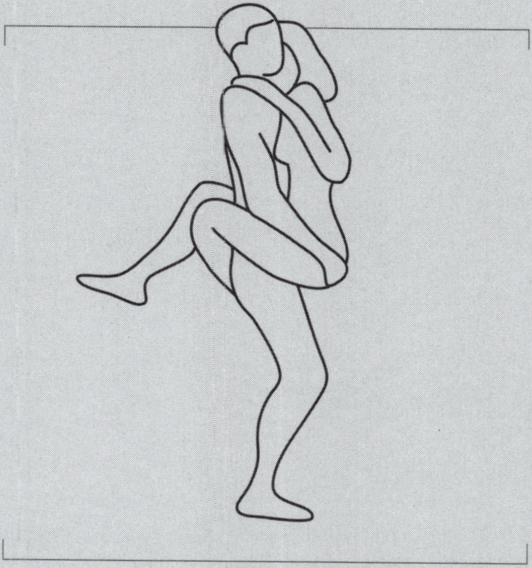

ONE SAUSAGE WRAP, TO GO

january.) 25

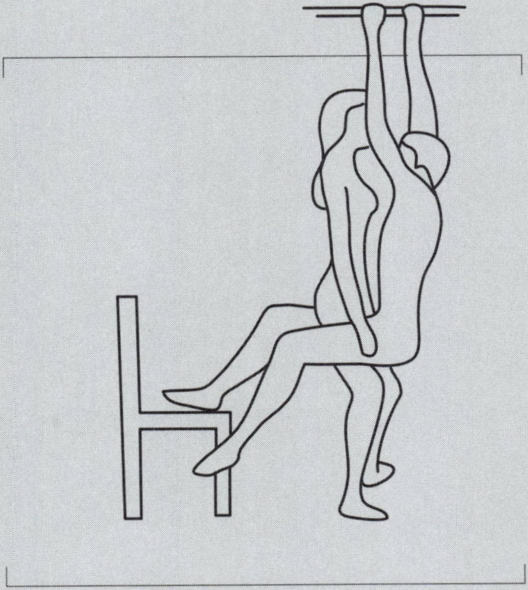

THE PULL-UP

january.) **26**

THE PAS DE DEUX

january.)

27

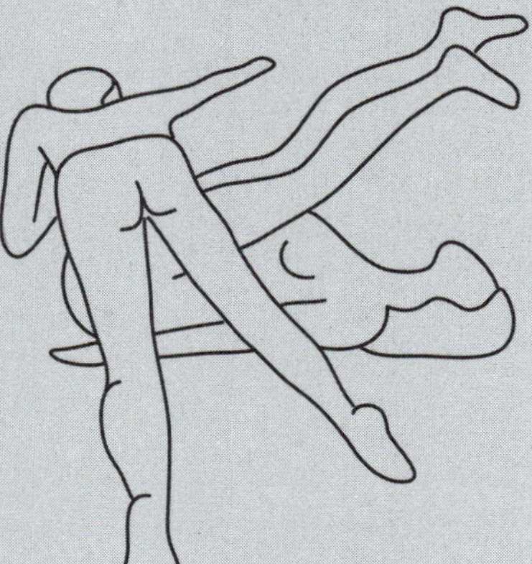

THE SHORT STACK

january.) **28**

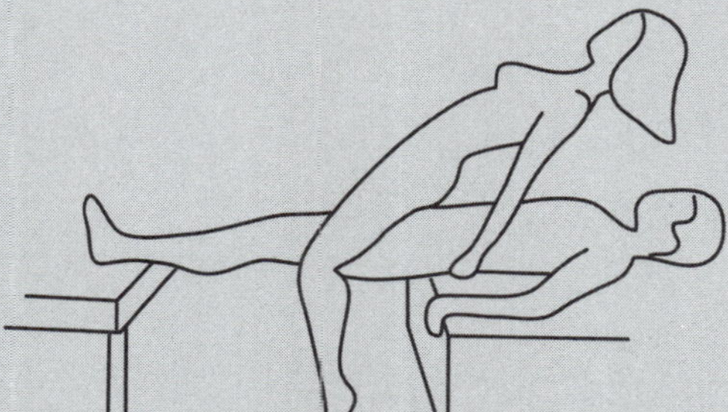

THE MOTION SIMULATION RIDE

january.) 29

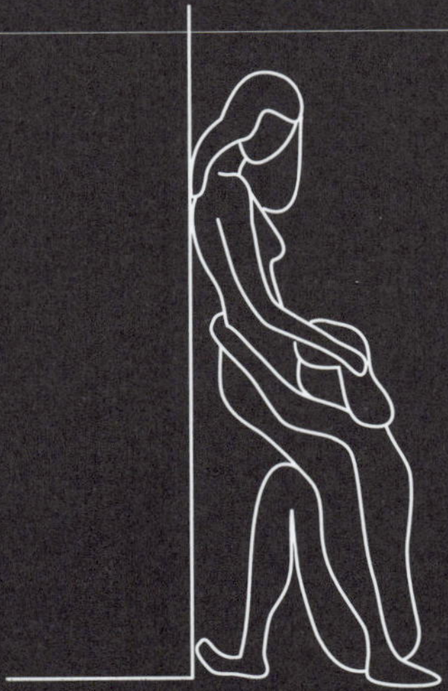

THE DOWN COMFORTER

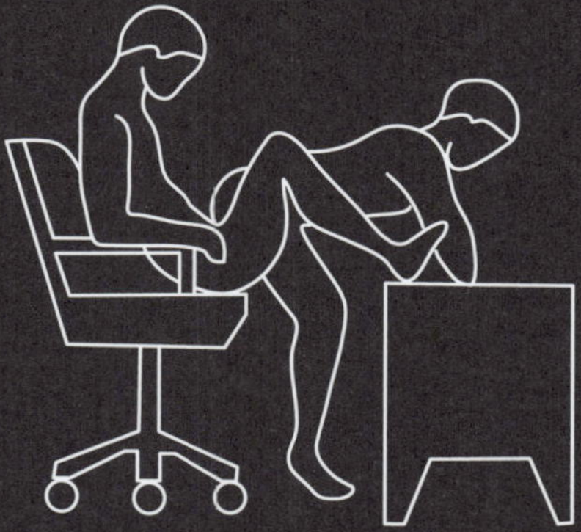

THE DESKTOP

january.)

31

THE TUNNEL OF LOVE

february.) **01**

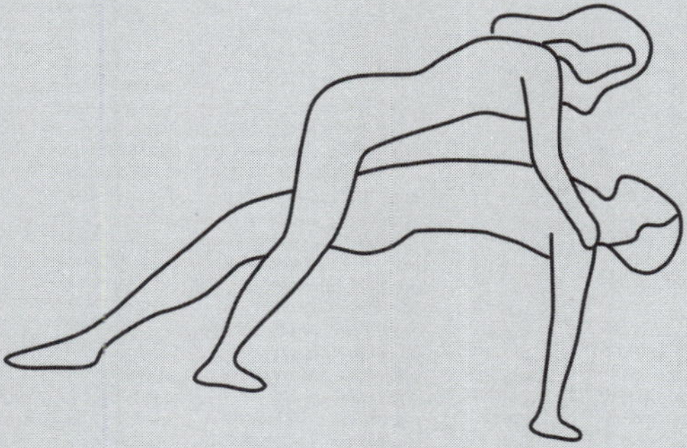

THE DOUBLE RAINBOW

february.)

02

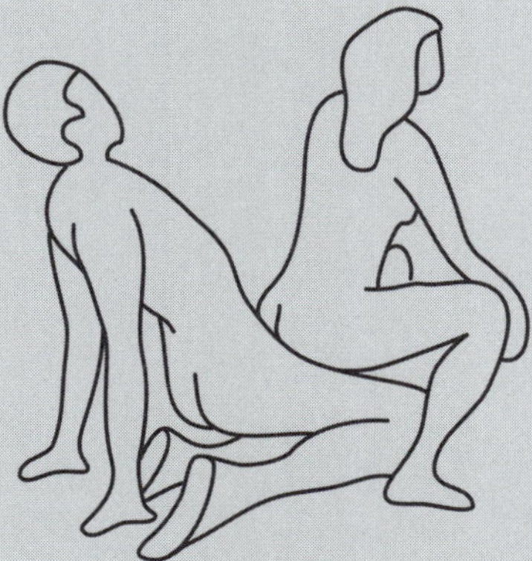

WHAT ARE YOU, MY SHADOW?

february.)

03

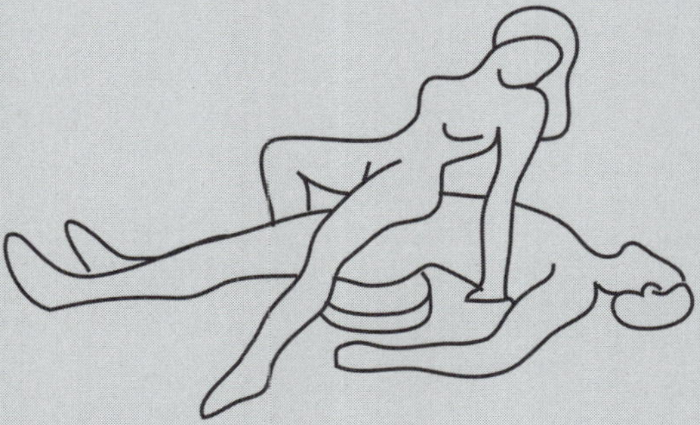

THE STEALTH BOMBSHELL

february.) 04

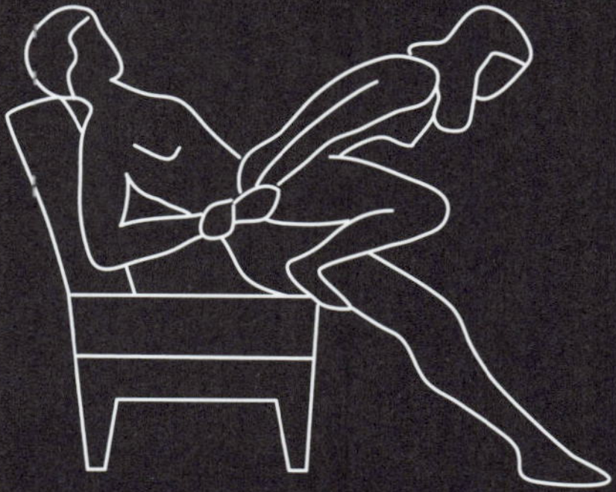

THE STARTING BLOCK

february.)

05

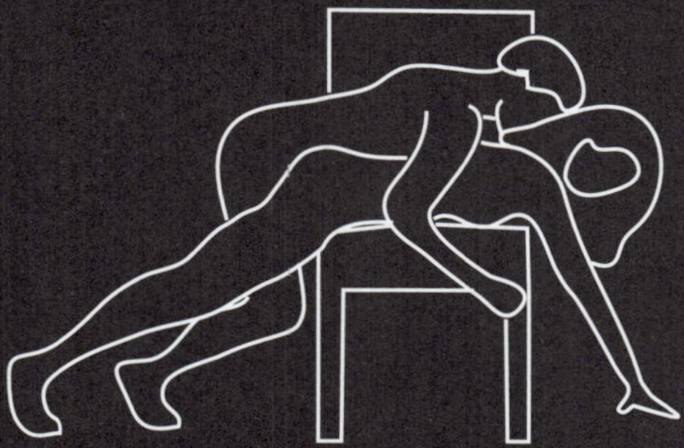

HELPING YOUR FRIEND MOVE

february.)

06

UNDER THE HOOD

february.)

07

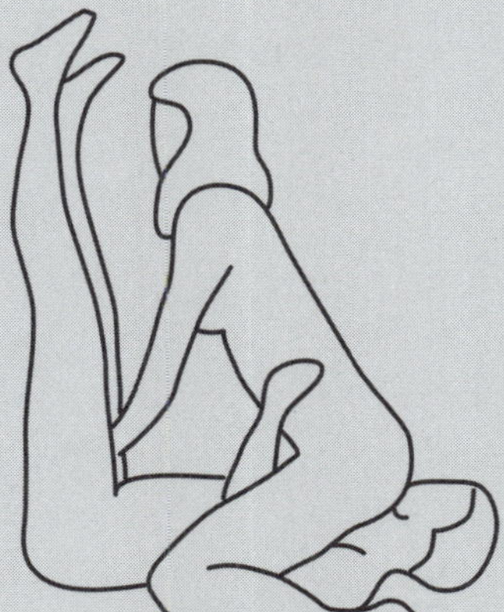

THE BOTTOM FEEDER

february.)

08

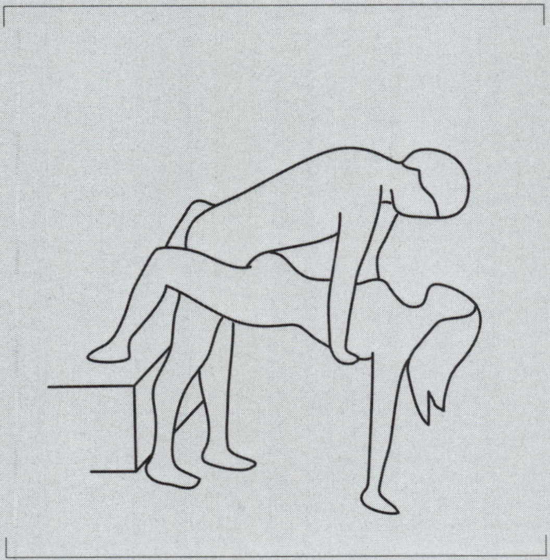

THE FRENCH DIP

february.)

09

ELBOW ROOM

february.) 10

THE HALF HITCH

february.)

11

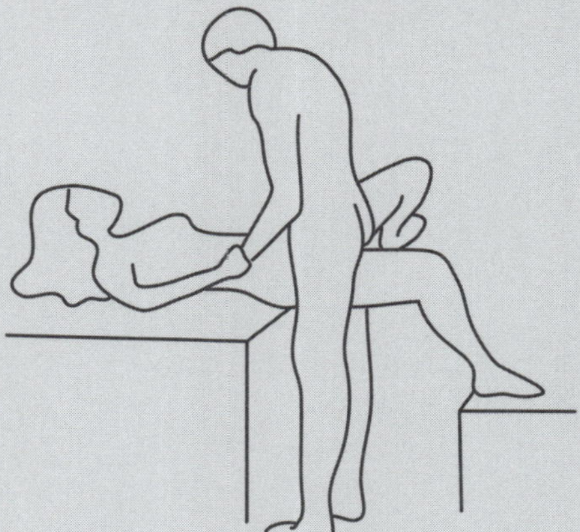

SEXUAL HEELING

february.)

12

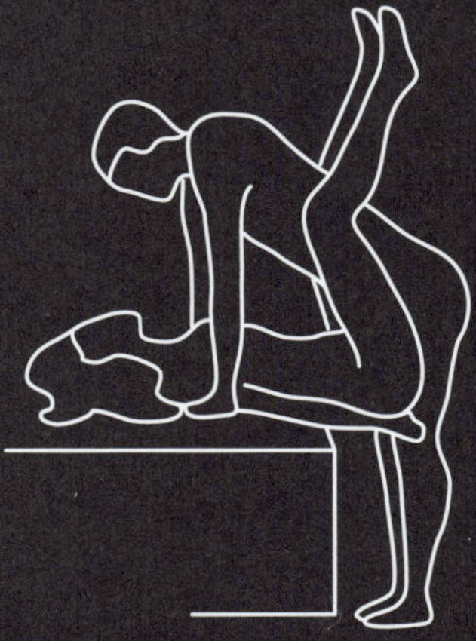

TAKE THE EDGE OFF

THE DOWN UNDER

february.) **14**

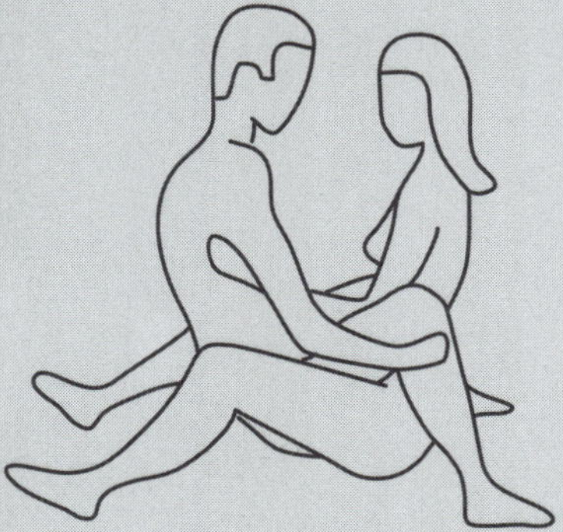

MY CUP OF TEA

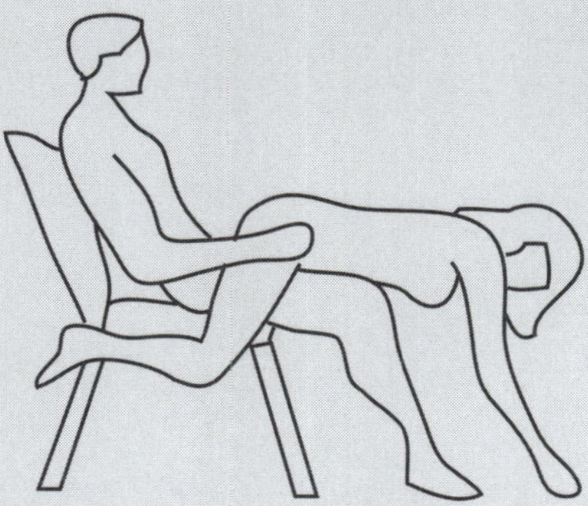

THE BACK SEAT DRIVER

february.) 16

THE FLYING BUTT PLIERS

february.) **17**

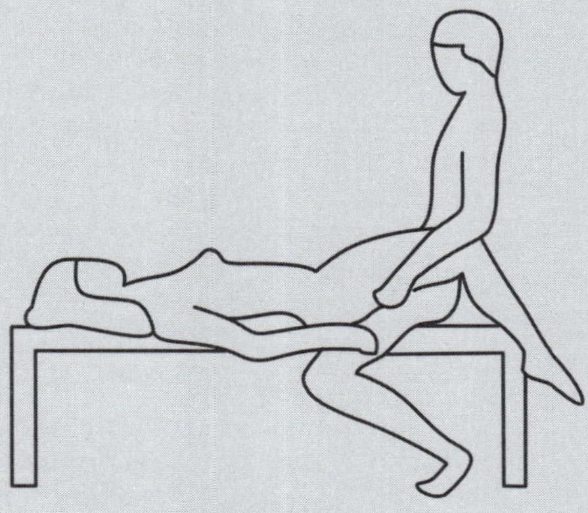

RIDE THE BENCH

february.) 18

THE POWER HOUR

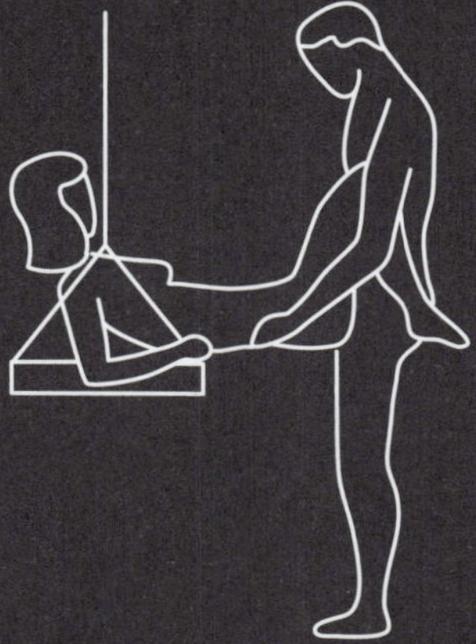

SWINGERS

february.)

20

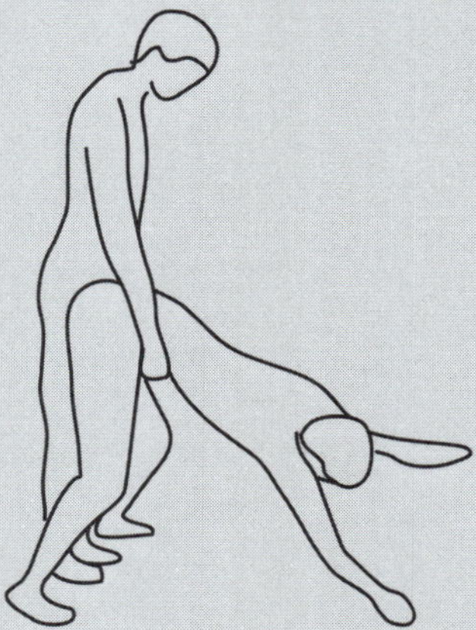

THE YOGA BUDDY

february.) 21

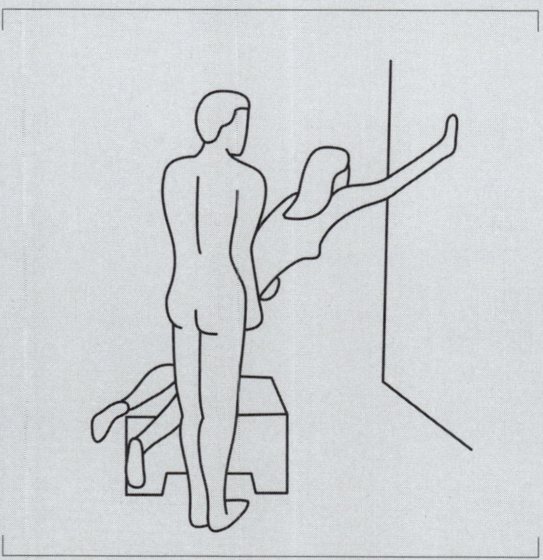

RAISING THE ROOF

february.)

22

THE SIDEWINDER

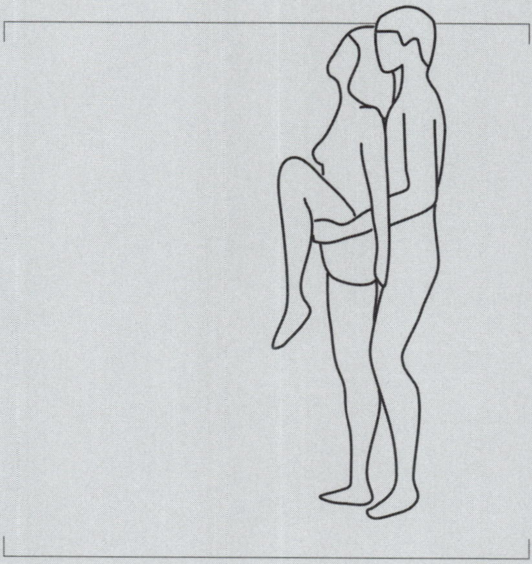

THE KNEE HIGH

february.) 24

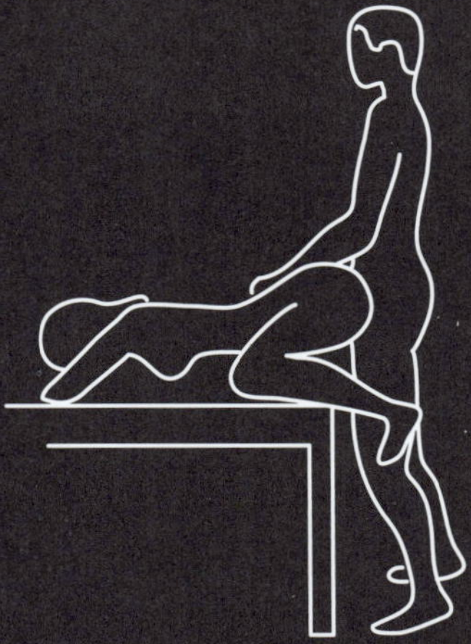

ON THE LEVEL

february.)

25

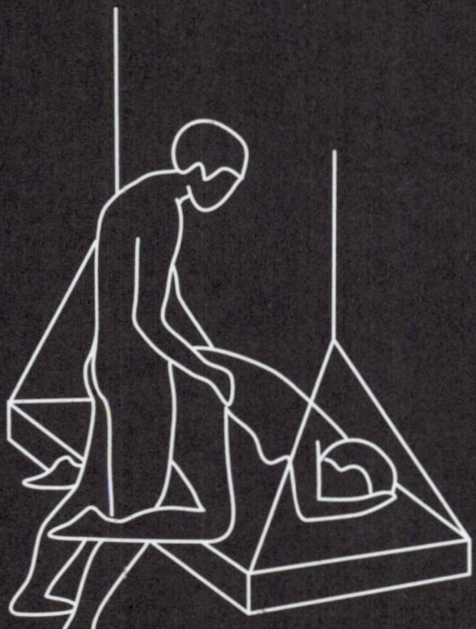

THE BIG SWING

february.) 26

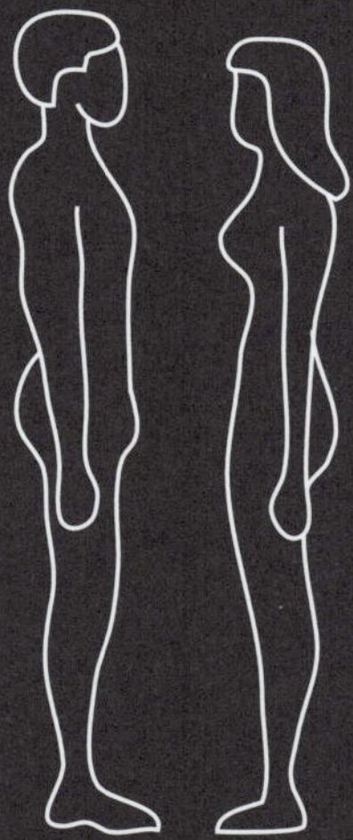

THE EYE TO EYE

I CAN SEE MY HOUSE FROM HERE

february.)

28

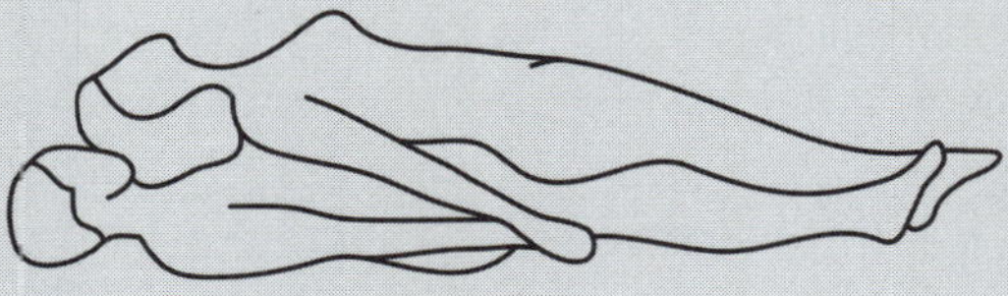

THE LOW-KEY

february.)

29

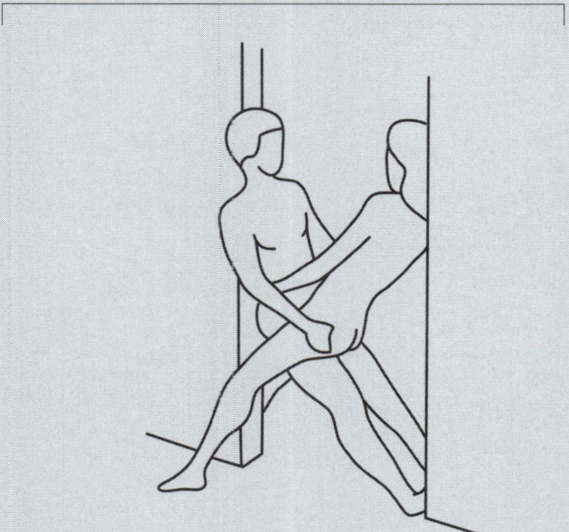

THE DOOR JAM

march.)

01

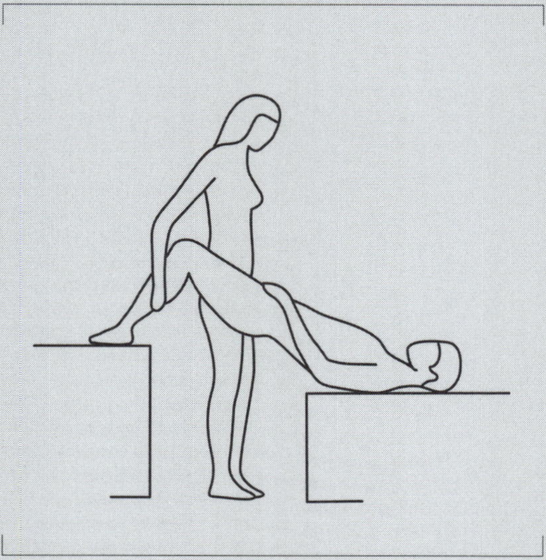

THE ESCALATOR

march.) **02**

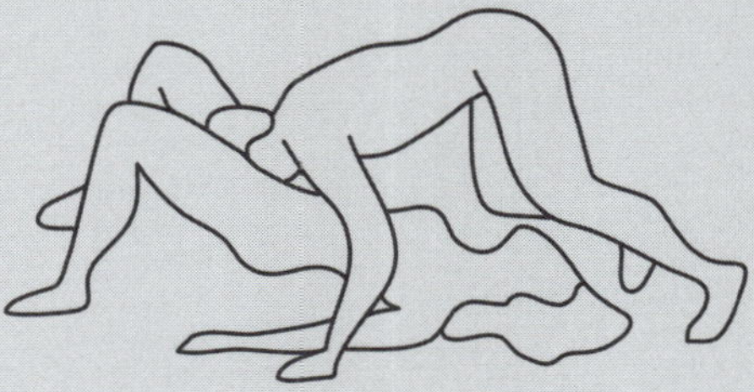

THE ABDOMINIZER

march.) **03**

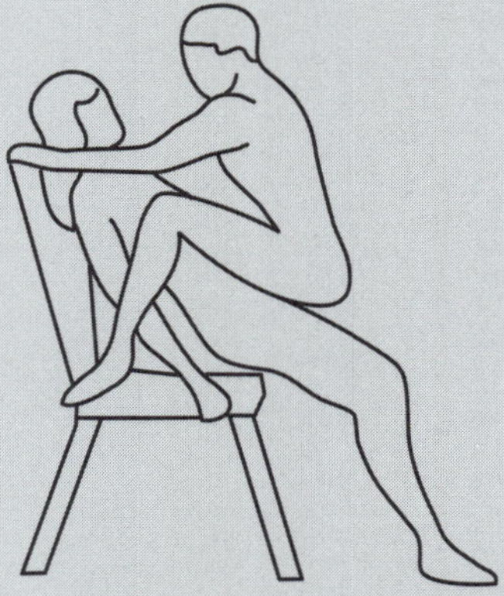

IT'S TIME FOR MY WALK

march.) **04**

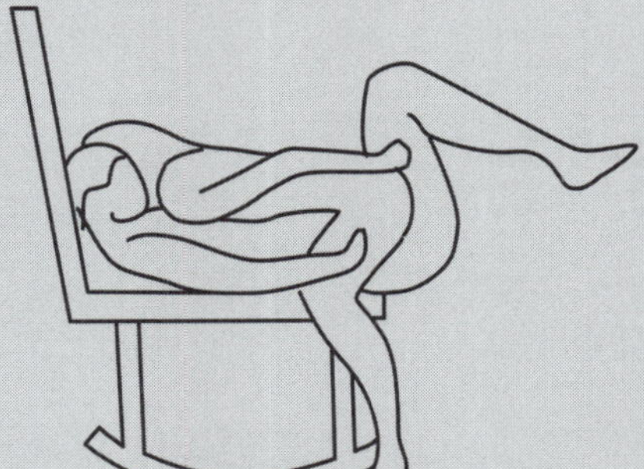

THE SNACK CAKE

march.) **05**

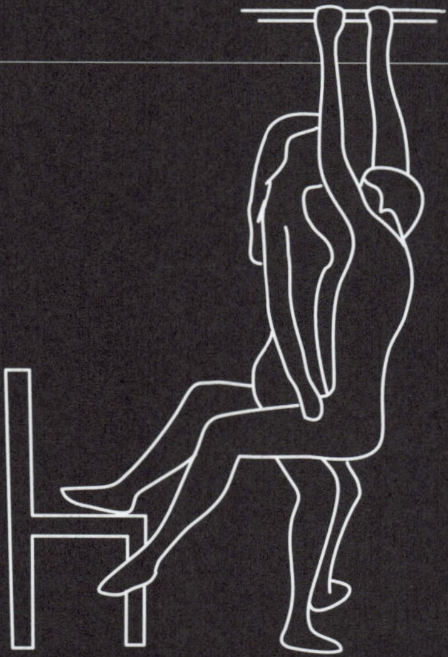

THE HUNGMAN

march.) **06**

THE CHAIN OF FOOLS

march.)

07

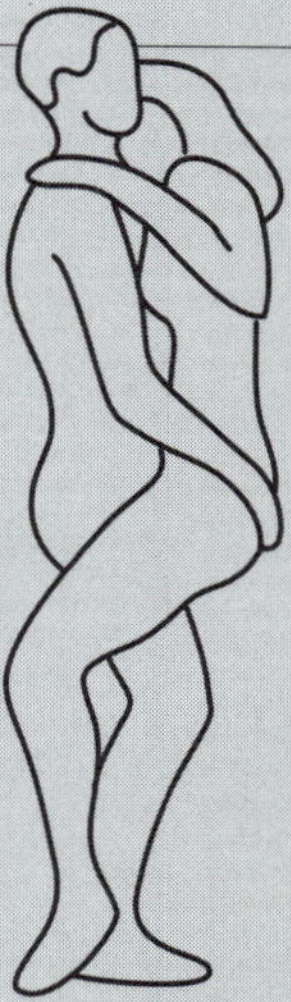

CLOSE QUARTERS

march.) 08

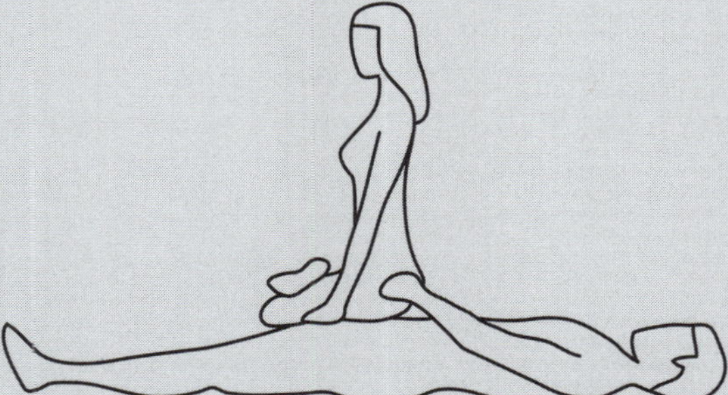

SITTING ON TOP OF THE WORLD

march.) 09

THE GLADIATOR

march.)

10

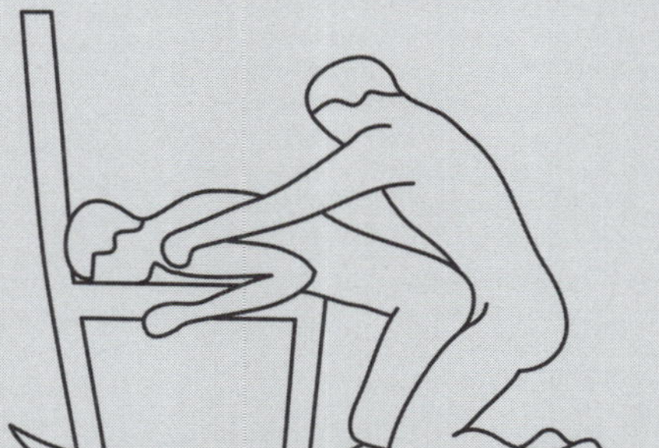

THE CONSOLATION

march.)

11

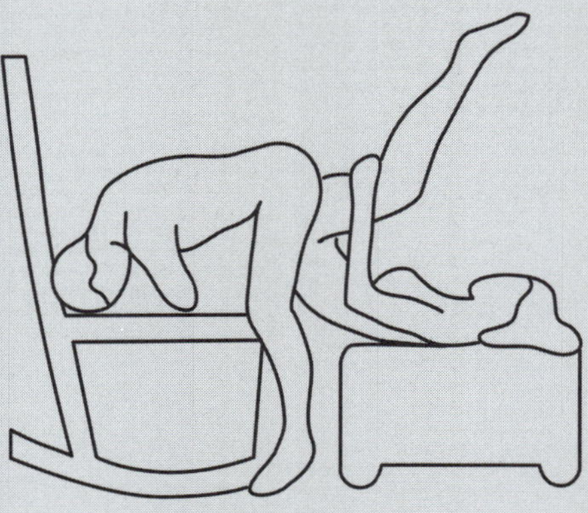

THE BENEFITS OF STRETCHING

march.)

12

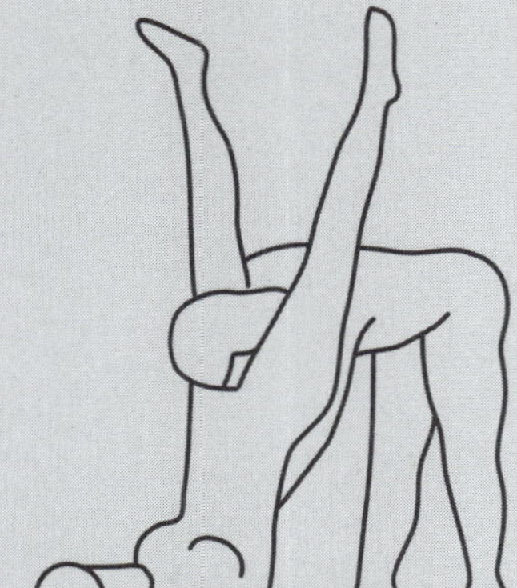

THE BIRDFEEDER

march.)

13

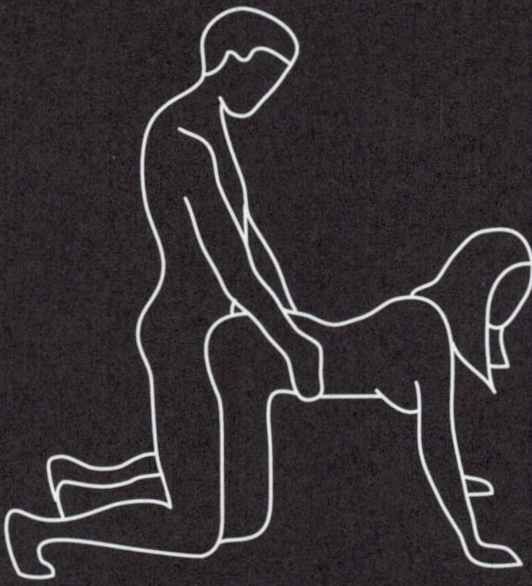

THE OLD RELIABLE

march.) **14**

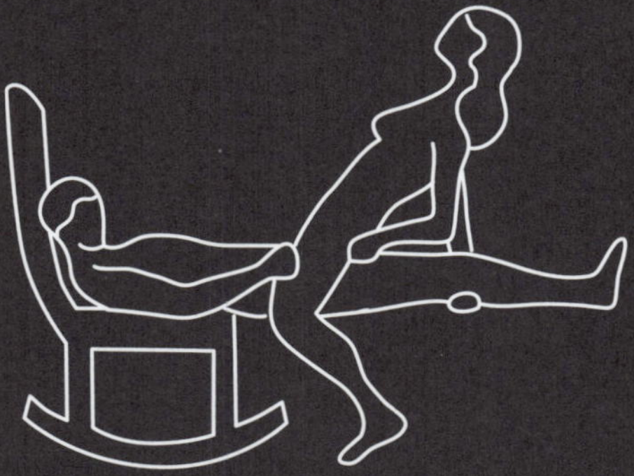

THE HOVERCRAFT

march.) **15**

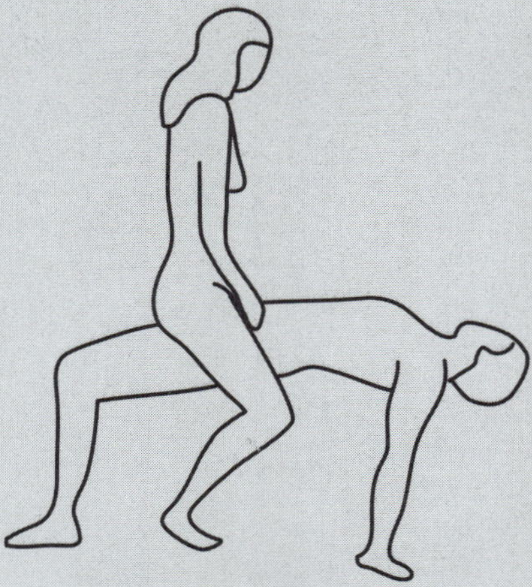

THE TABLE DANCE

march.)

16

THE TANDEM CARTWHEEL

march.)

17

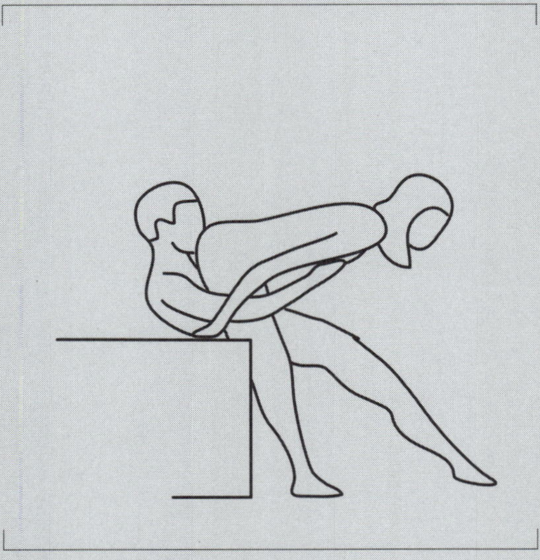

THE RIMSHOT

march.)

18

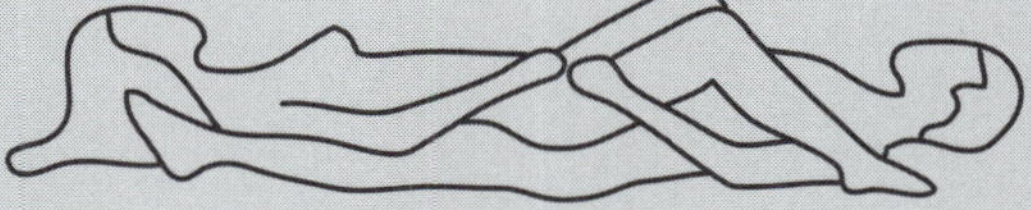

THE BADLANDS

march.)

19

THE LEG WARMER

march.) 20

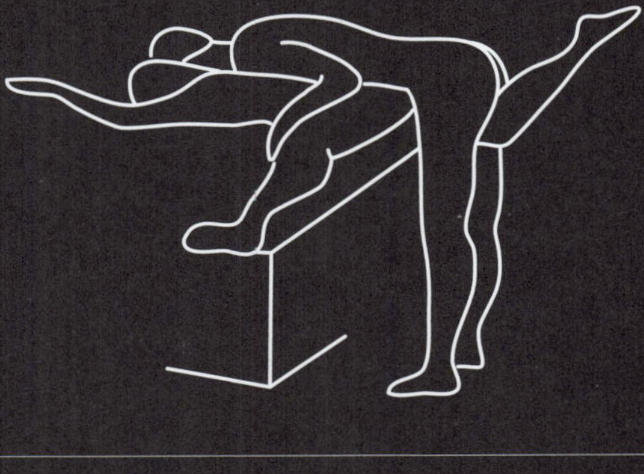

THE TAILFEATHER

march.)

21

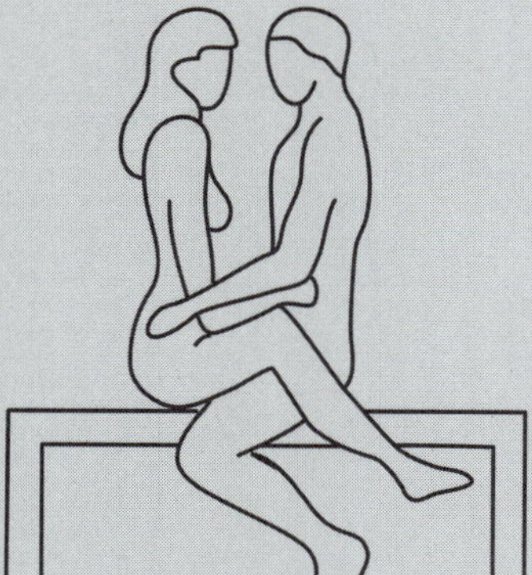

THE BENCH WARMERS

march.) **22**

THE STANDING O

march.)

23

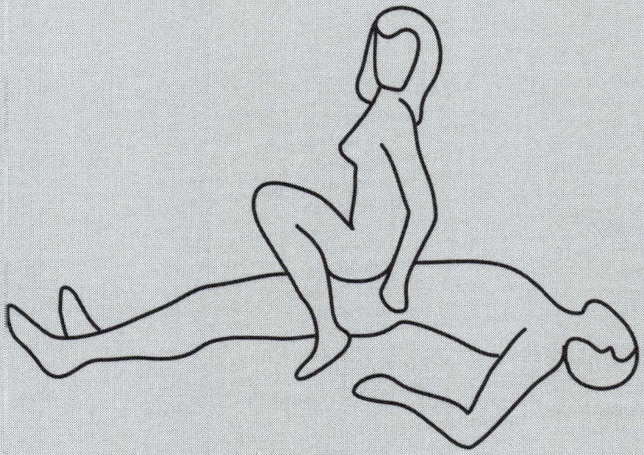

THE SIT & SPIN

march.) 24

THE HUMPBACK WAIL

march.) **25**

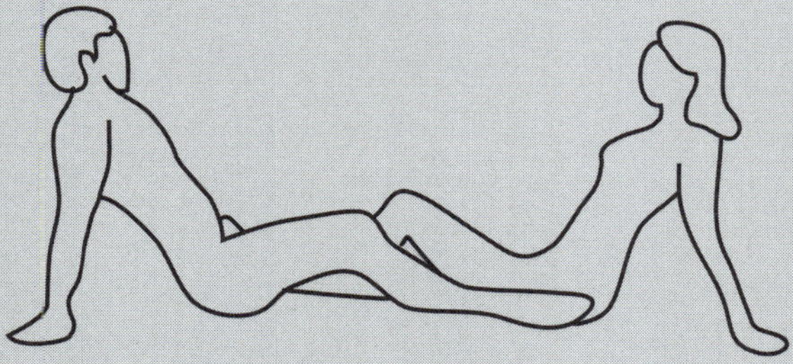

THE PRUDE AWAKENING

march.)

26

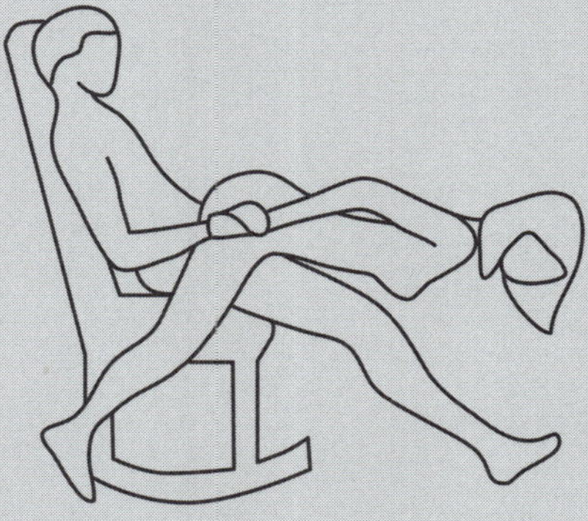

THE MOTION OF THE OCEAN

march.) 27

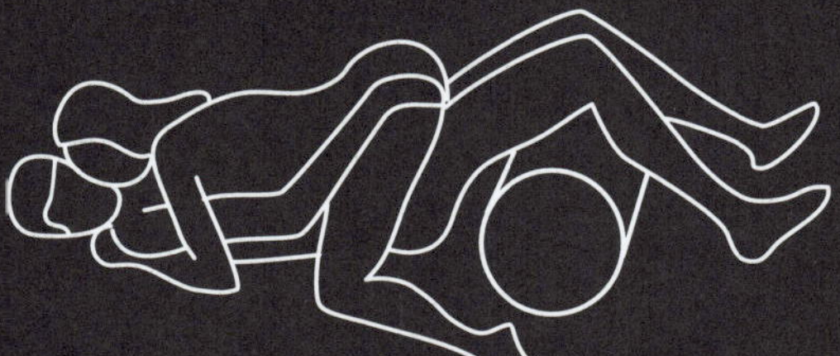

ROLL WITH IT

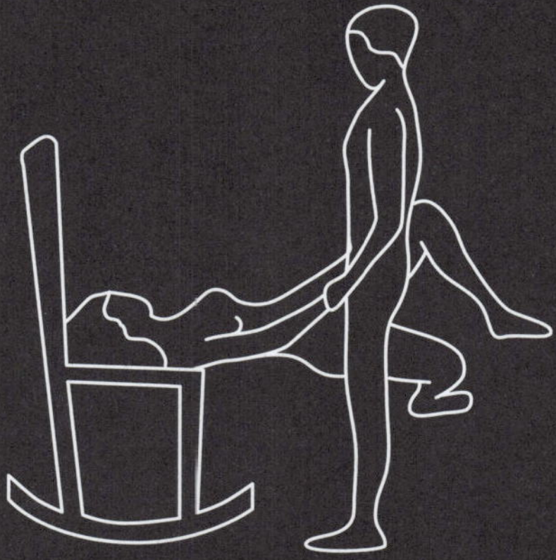

THE PUBIC PENDULUM

march.) 29

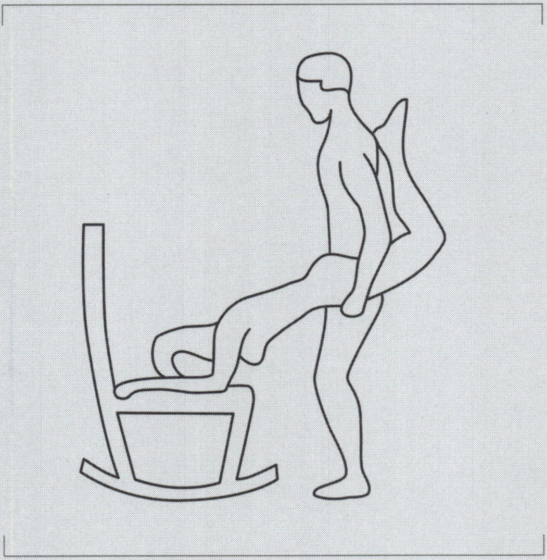

THE NOSE DIVE

march.) **30**

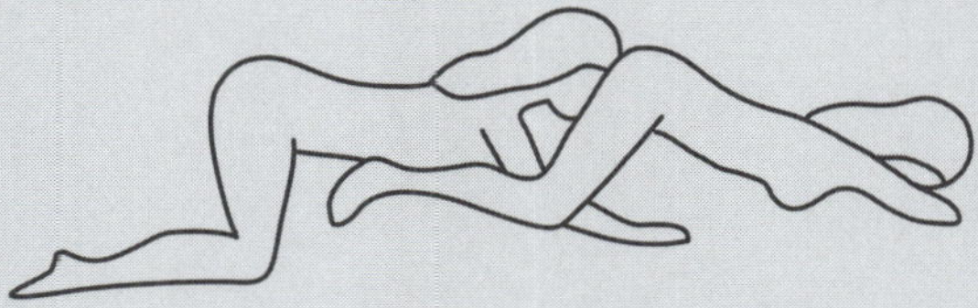

BASIC INSTINCT

march.)

31

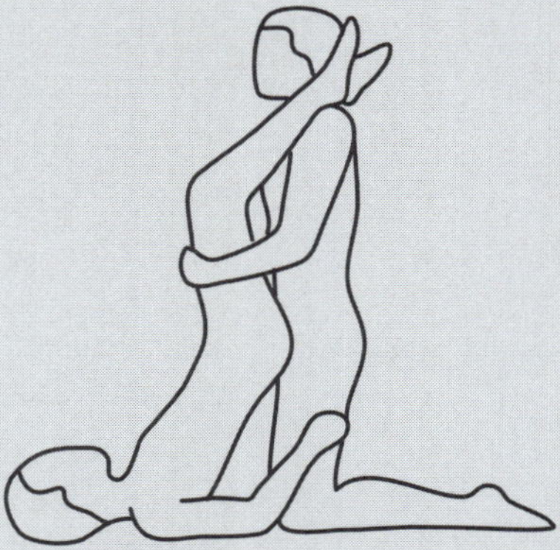

THE PILE DRIVER

april.) **01**

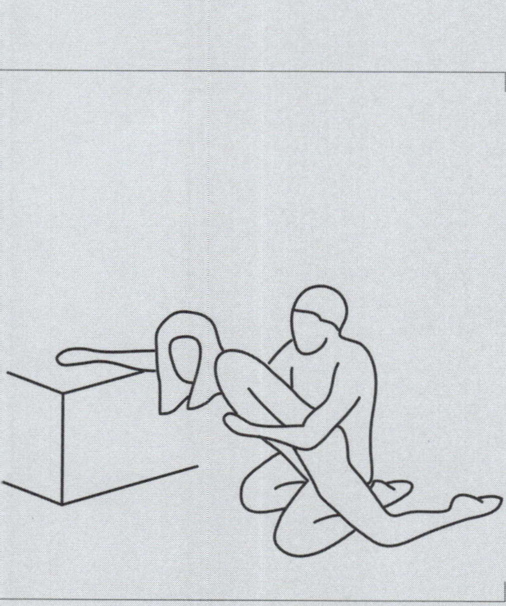

AN ARM AND A LEG

april.) **02**

THANKS FOR THE LIFT

THE TADPOLE

april.)

04

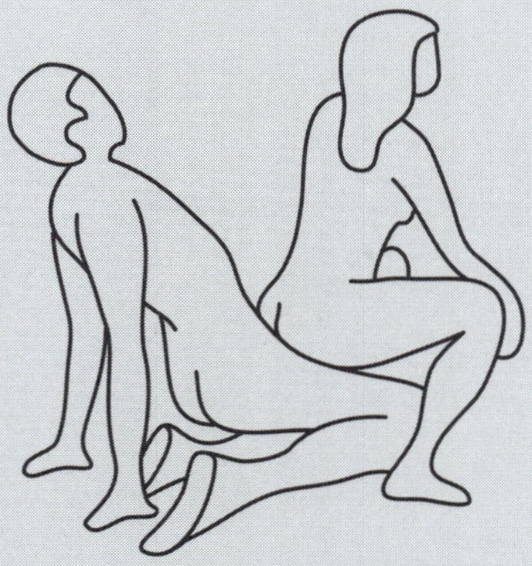

I LIKE TO WATCH

april.) **05**

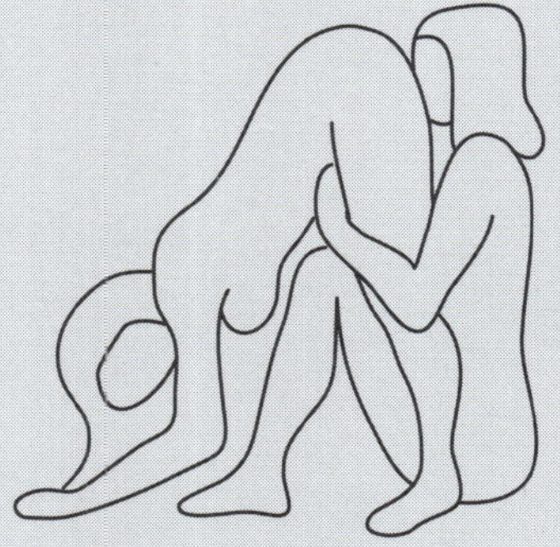

THE GETTING TO KNOW YOU

april.)

06

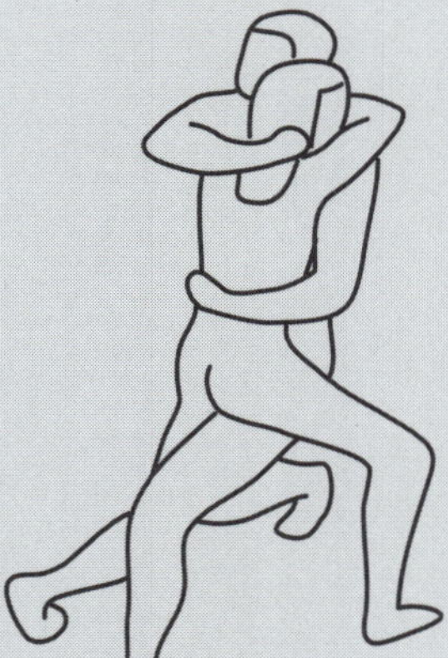

STRICTLY BEDROOM

april.) **07**

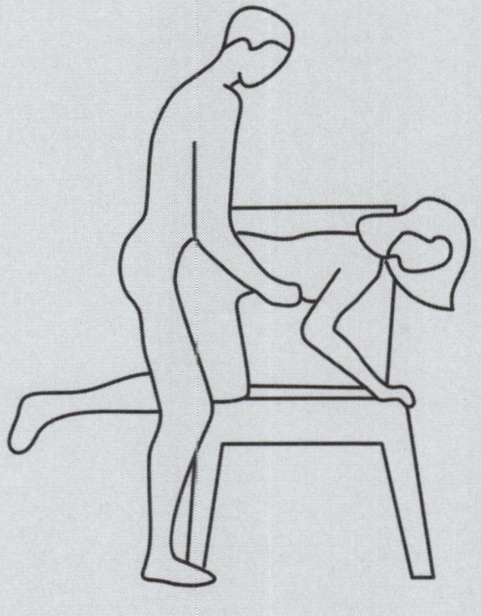

GRAB A CHAIR

april.) **08**

THE DISMOUNT

april.)

09

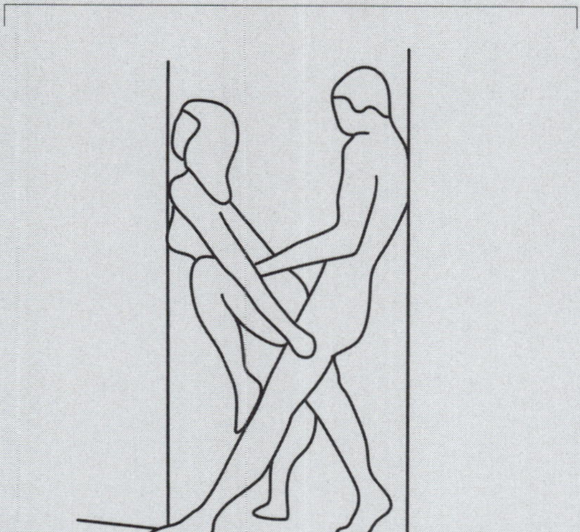

THE FRAME JOB

april.) **10**

LOOKING FOR LOOSE CHANGE

april.) **11**

BACK IN BUSINESS

april.)

12

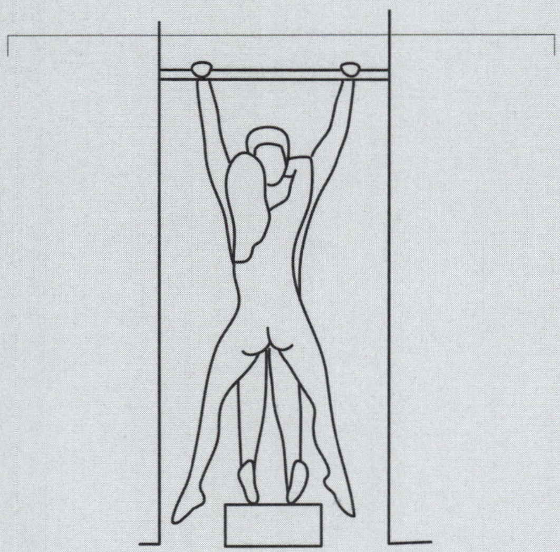

PULL OUTS

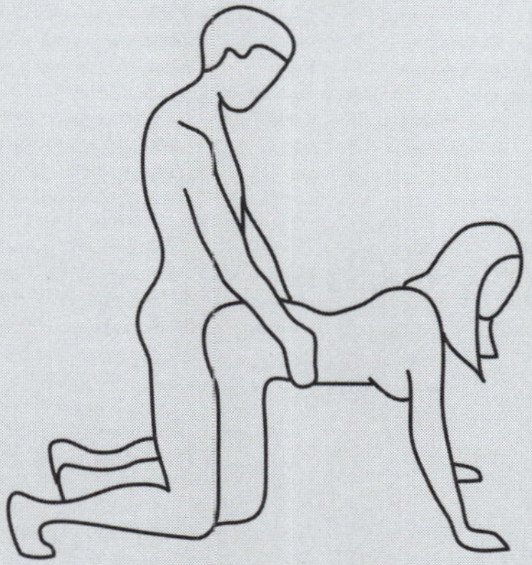

THE ALL IN

april.)

14

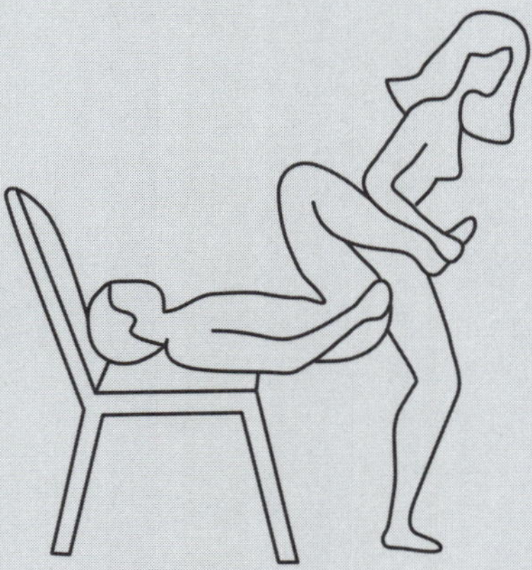

THE RICKSHAW

april.)

15

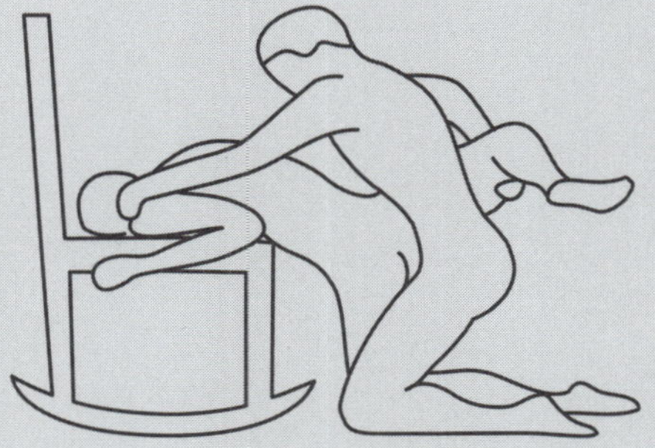

ROW THE BOAT

april.) 16

THE JAWS OF LIFE

april.)

17

THE BRICKLAYER

april.) **18**

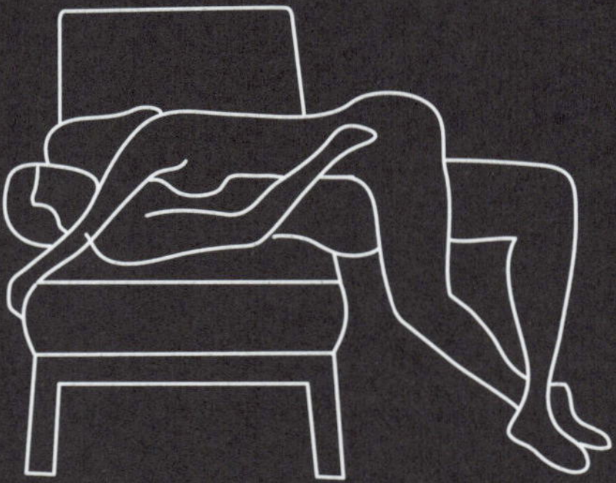

THE BELLY FLOP

april.) **19**

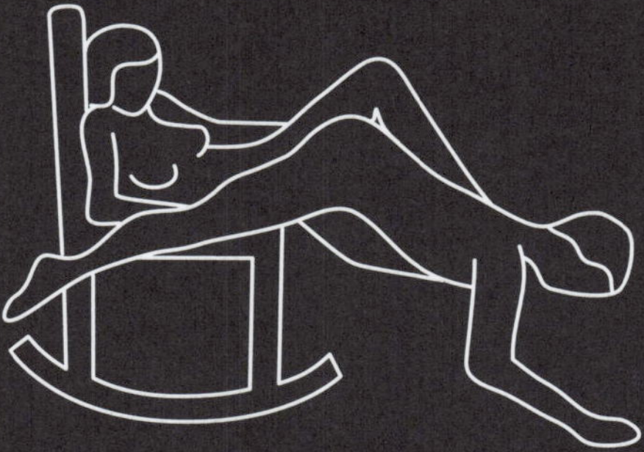

I'M SLIPPING . . .

april.) **20**

THE DRILL BIT

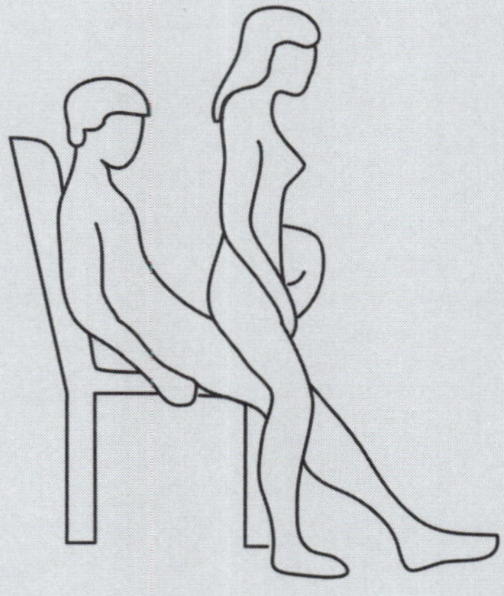

IS THIS SEAT TAKEN?

april.) **22**

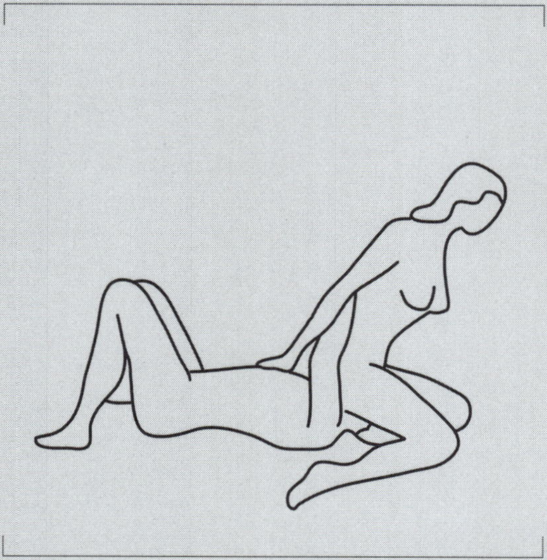

THE MUZZLE

april.) 23

THE BACKPACK

april.)

24

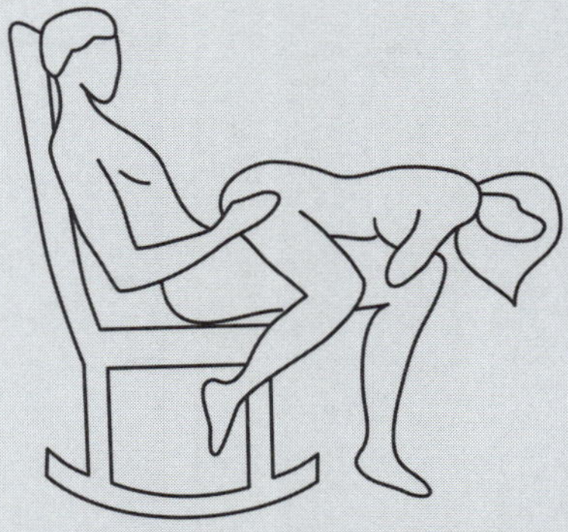

OFF TO THE RACES

90 AND RISING

april.) 26

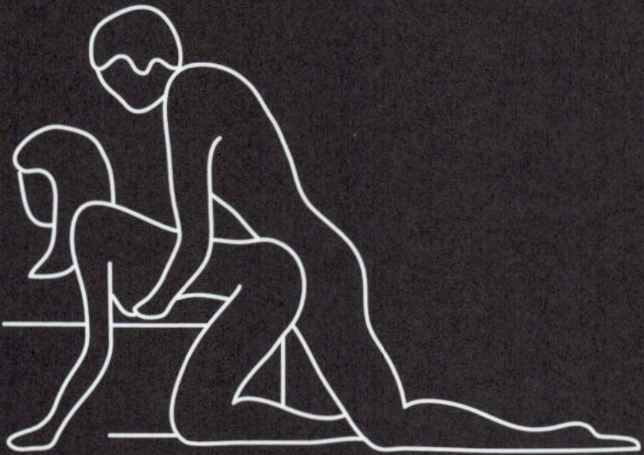

THE HEIMLICH

april.) **27**

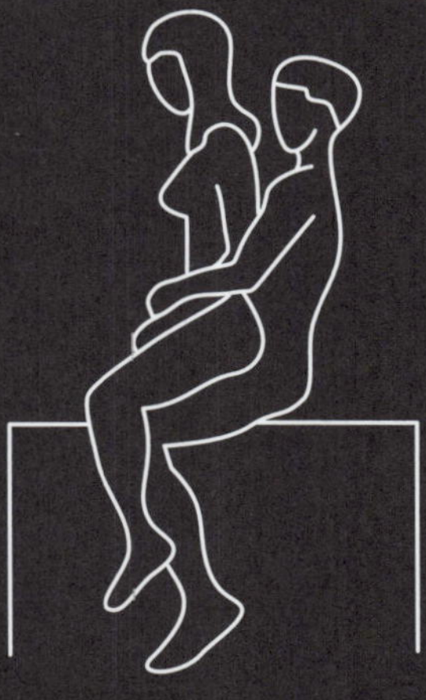

THE BUMPY RIDE

april.) 28

GET YOUR KICKS

april.) 29

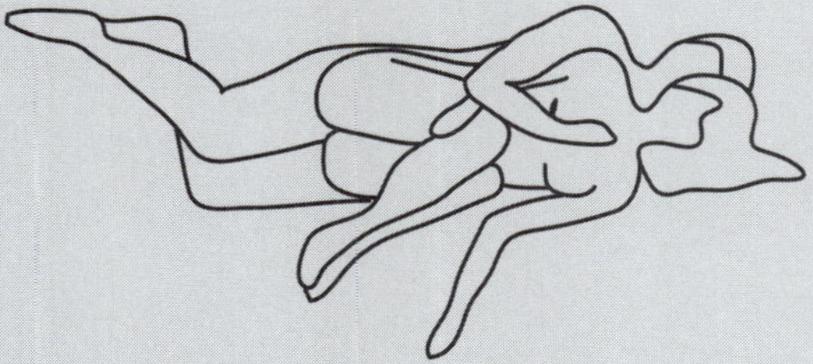

THE STOP, DROP & ROLL

april.) 30

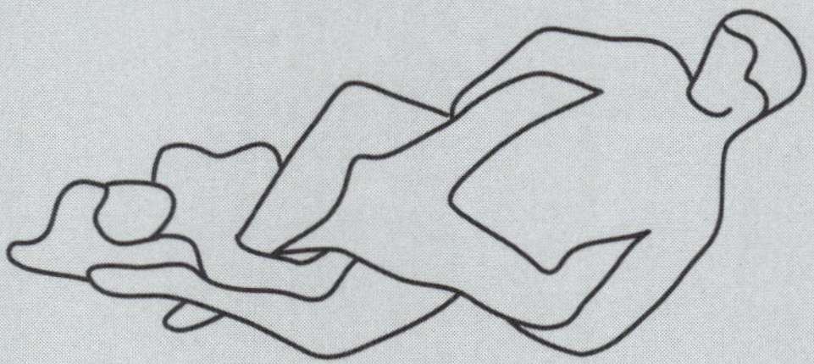

THE ESCHER

may.)

01

THE MAY POLE

may.) 02

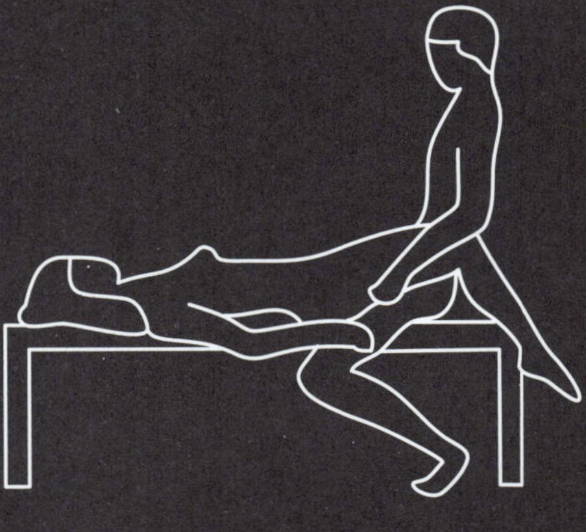

THE COFFEE TABLE HOOK

may.)

03

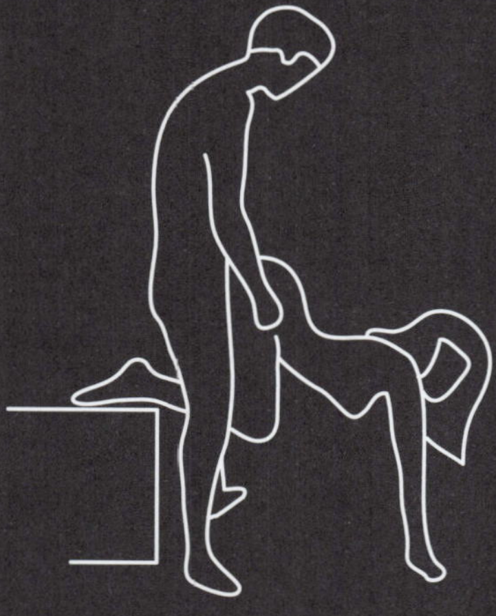

WOULD YOU STILL LOVE ME IF I WAS A WORM?

may.) **04**

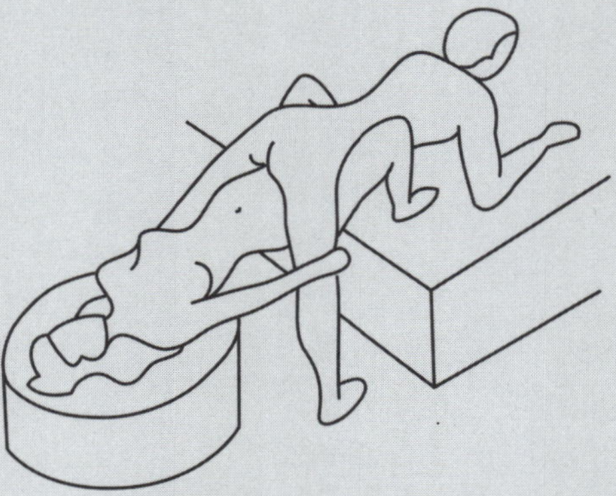

MISSIONARY IMPOSSIBLE

may.) **05**

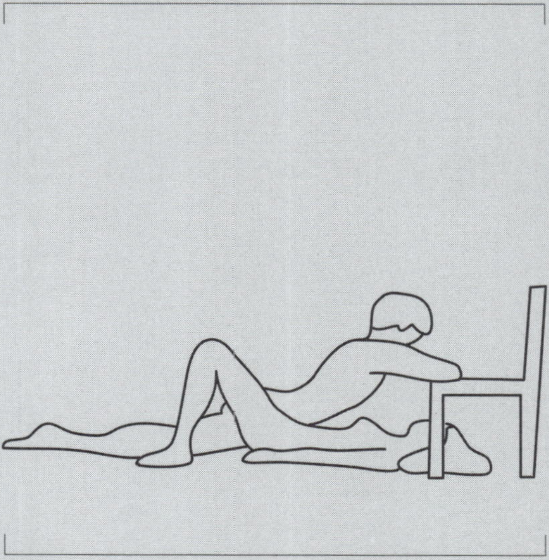

GUM INSPECTION

may.)

06

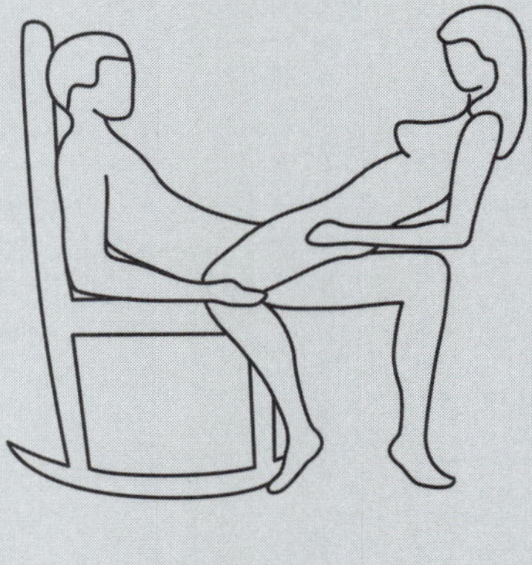

THE FUN HOUSE MIRROR

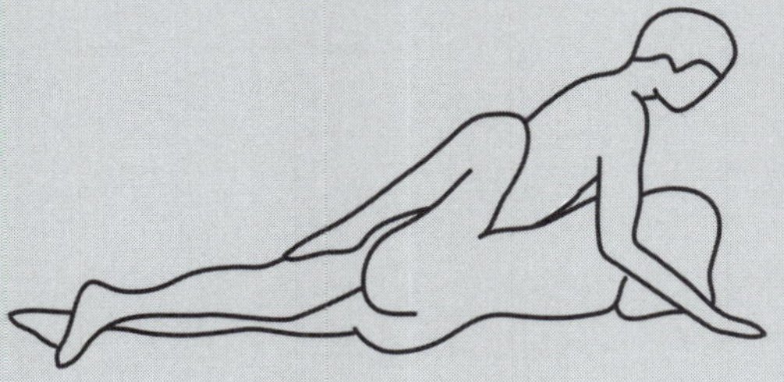

THE SIDE HUSTLE

may.)

08

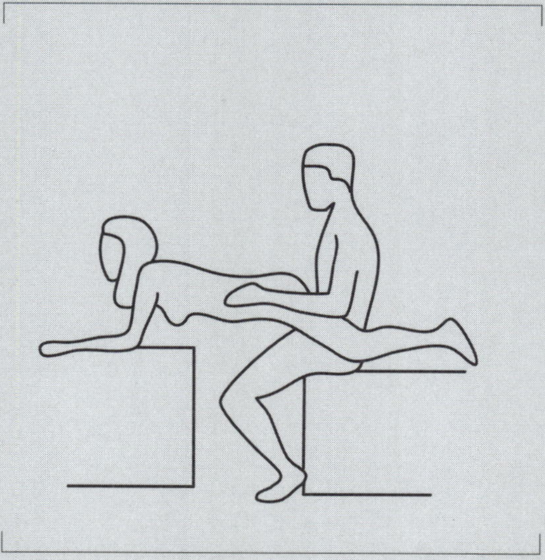

THE CORE WORKOUT

may.) 09

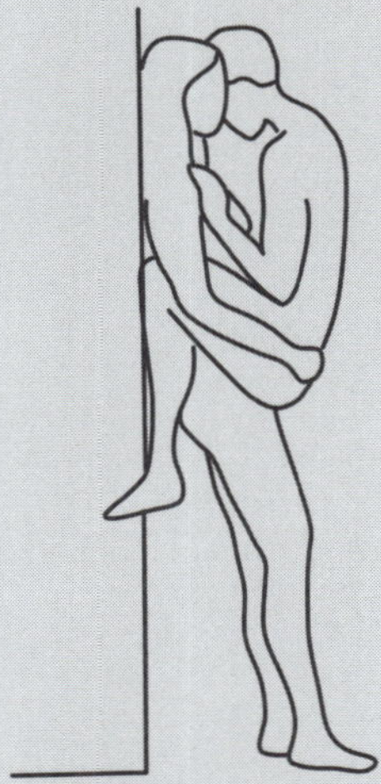

THE NO PANTS SLOW DANCE

may.) **10**

THE BRIGHT SIDE

may.) **11**

THE STROKE OF LUCK

may.)

12

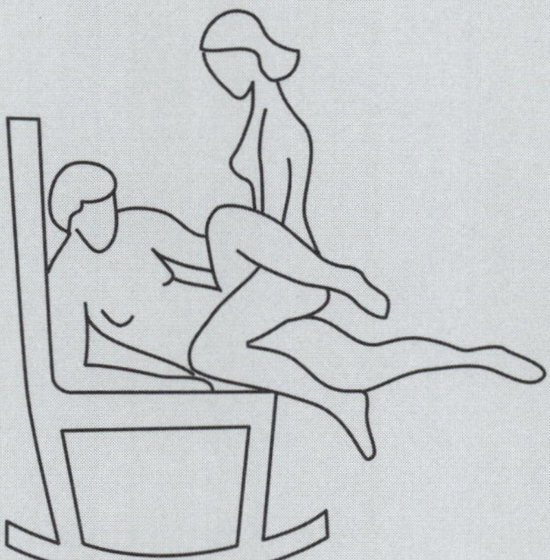

RIDE 'TIL YOU CAN'T NO MORE

may.)

13

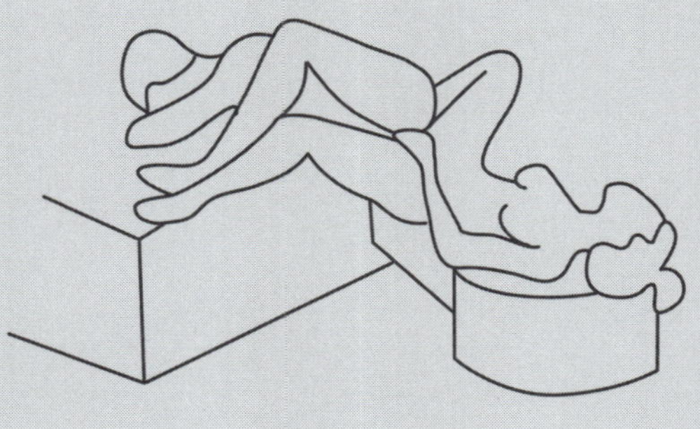

HOMEBIRTHING

may.)

14

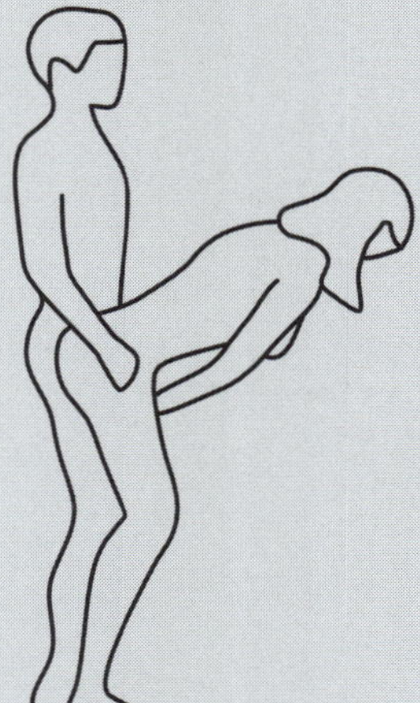

HIDING THE SALAMI

may.) **15**

THE LOWDOWN

may.) 16

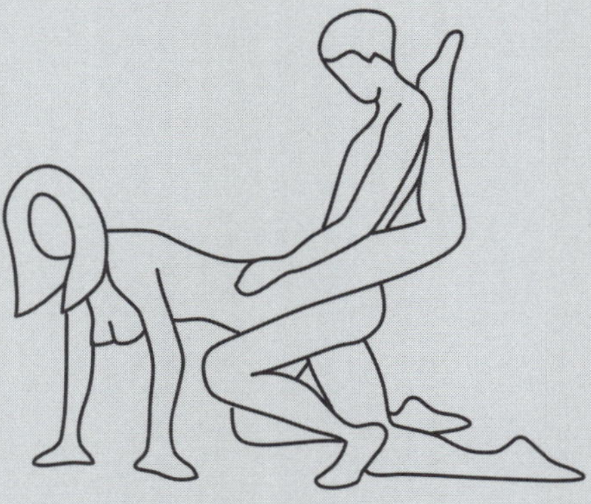

THE HIGH HEEL

may.)

17

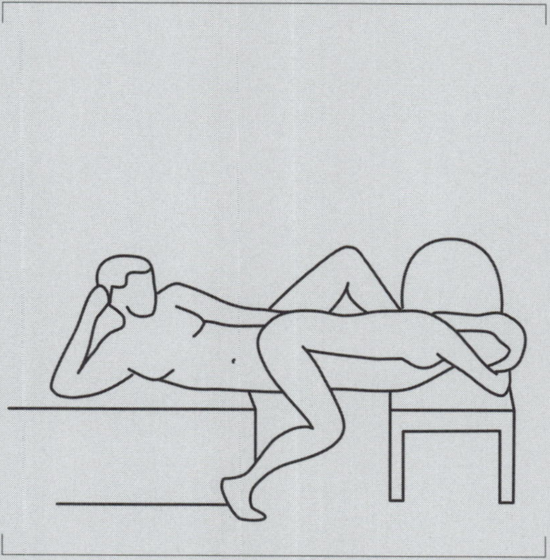

THE MICHELANGELO

may.) **18**

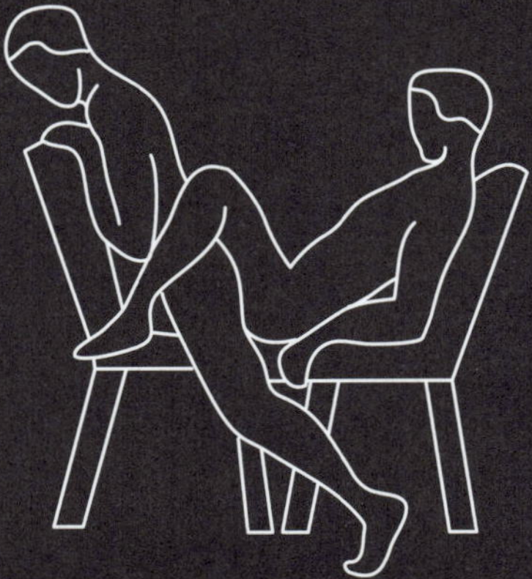

THE TWO-HUMPED DROMEDARY

may.) 19

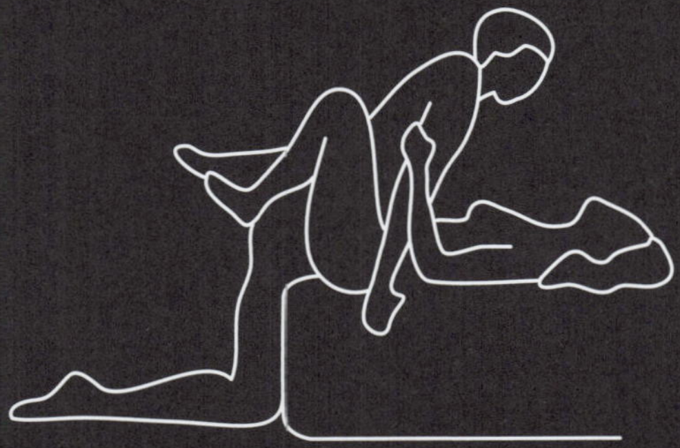

THE MATTRESS TEST

may.) 20

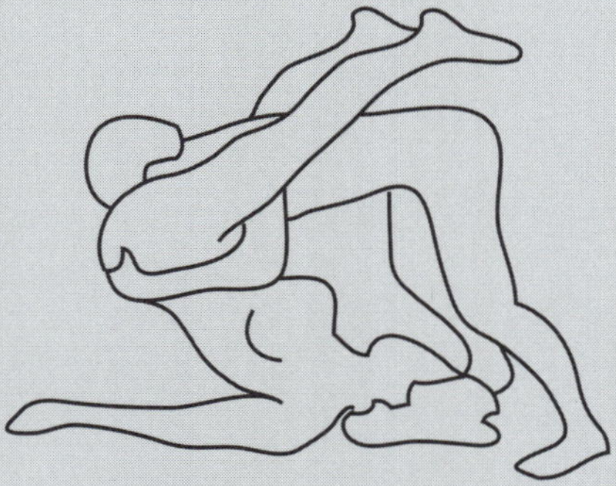

THE SIXTY-EIGHT

may.)

21

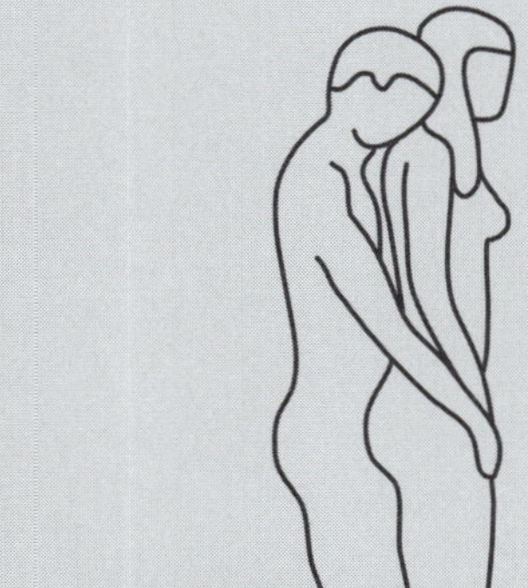

DOUBLECLICKING

may.) **22**

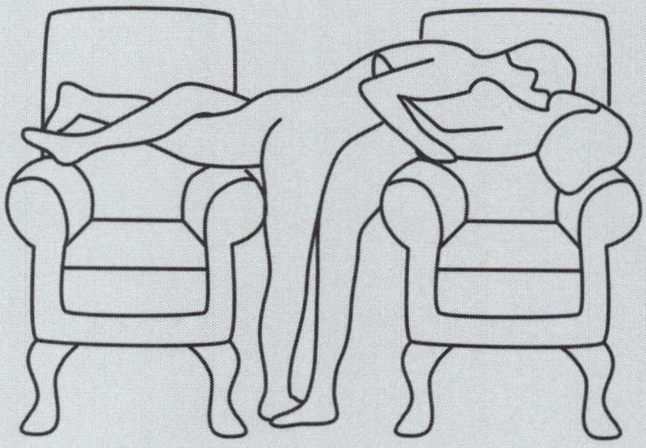

THE TWO-CHAIR SNARE

may.) **23**

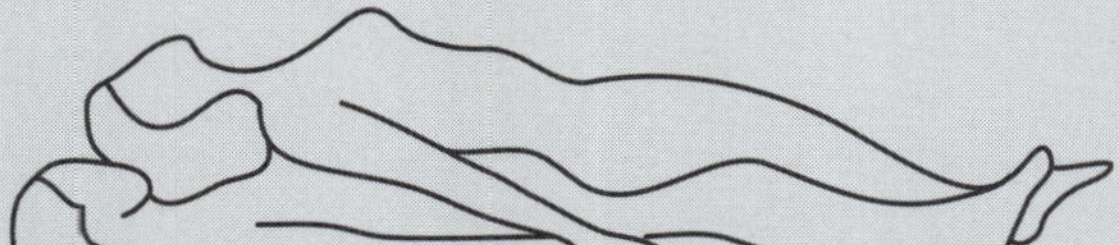

ALL THE FEELS

may.) **24**

THE TWO-RING CIRCUS

WHAT'S GOOD FOR THE GOOSE . . .

may.) 26

HUG IT OUT

may.)

27

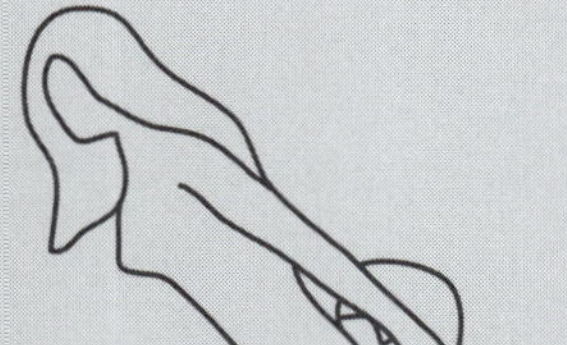

THE ASSASSIN

may.)

28

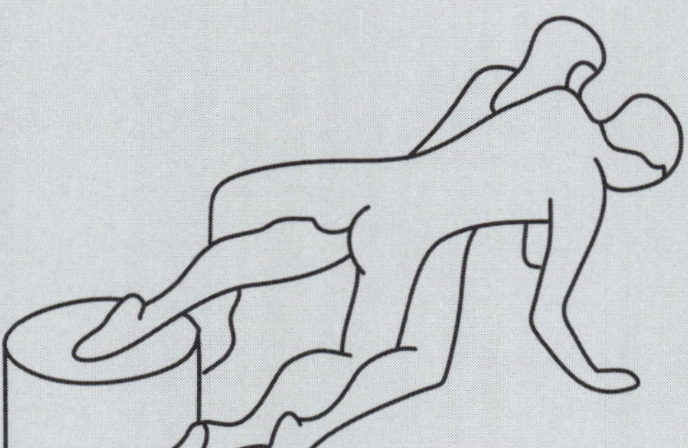

THE CLEAN TEAM

may.) 29

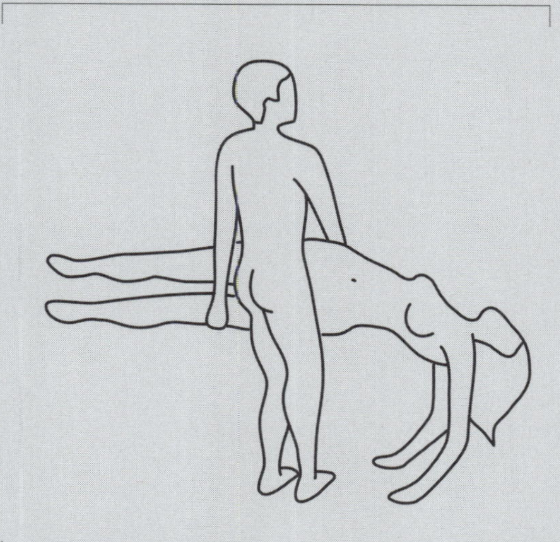

CARRIED AWAY

may.) **30**

THE STARING CONTEST

may.) **31**

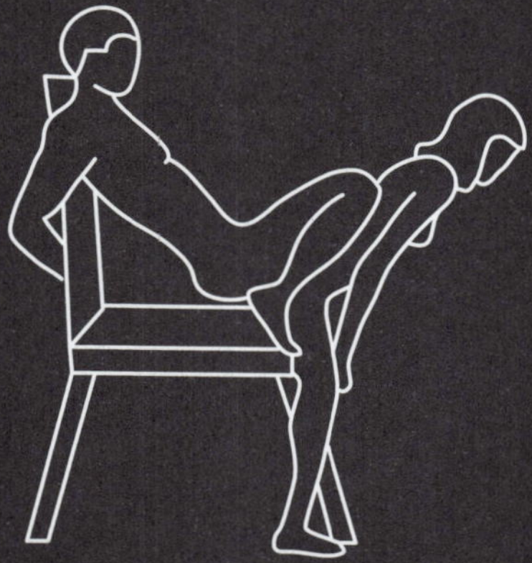

THE OLD TACK ON THE SEAT TRICK

june.)

01

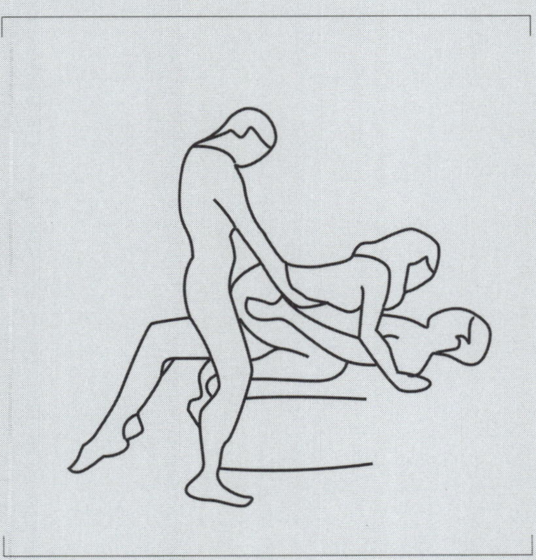

THE CLAMSHELL

june.)

02

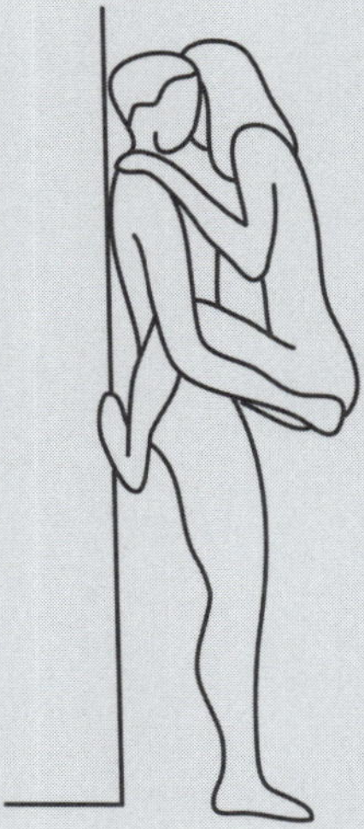

THE FULL FRONTAL

june.)

03

CHASING RAINBOWS

june.) **04**

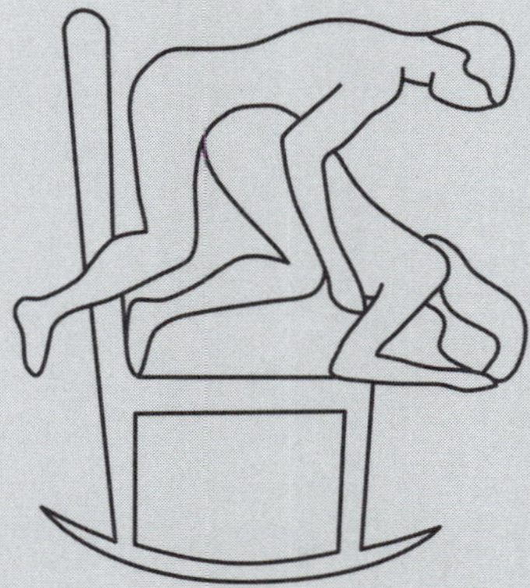

THE DOUBLE-DOGGY

june.)

05

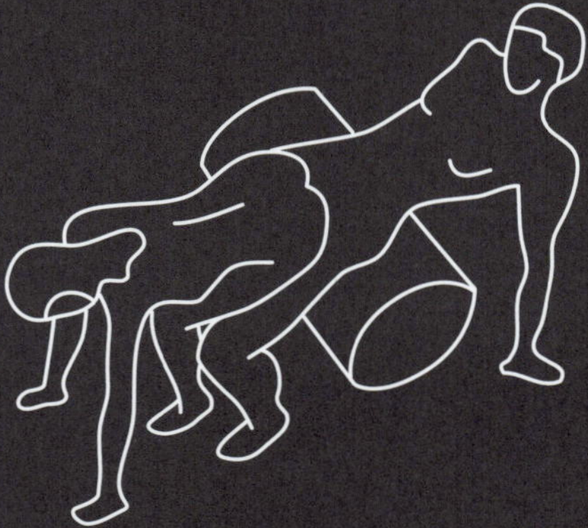

THE ROLLING PIN

june.)

06

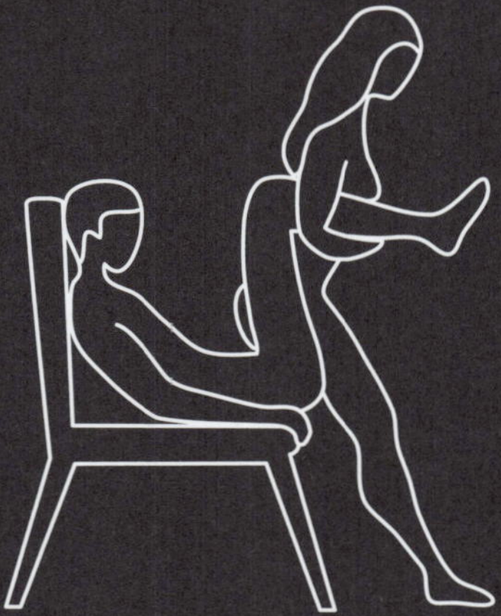

THE SLOUCH AND SIT

june.)

07

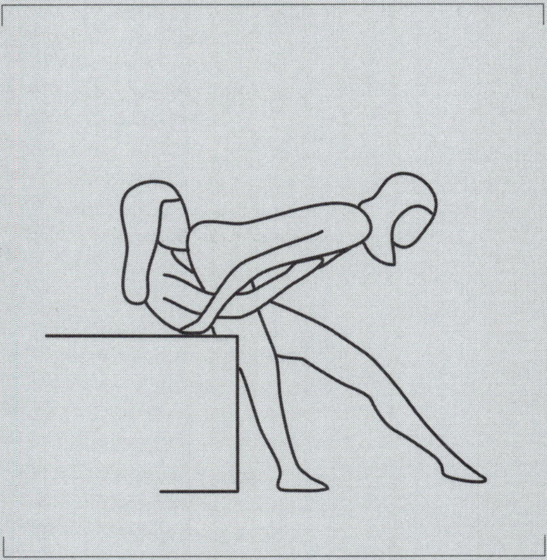

THE SLINGSHOT

june.) **08**

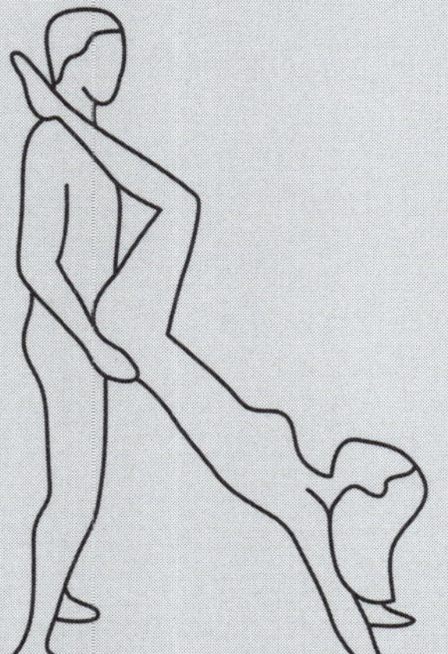

THE BEST OF TIMES, THE WORST OF TIMES

june.)

09

YOU GIVE ME FEMUR

june.)

10

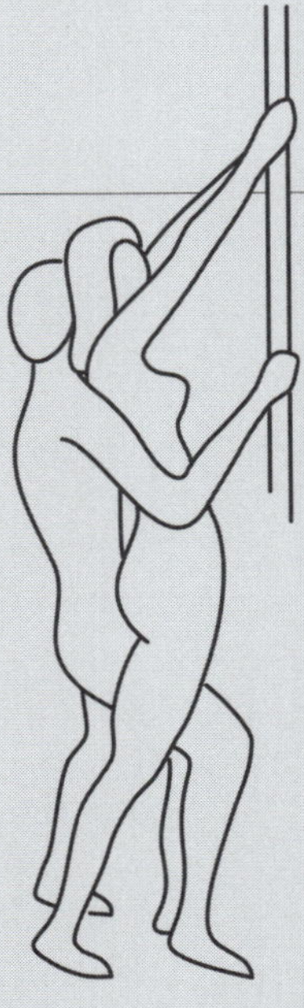

TARZAN, MEET JANE

june.) 11

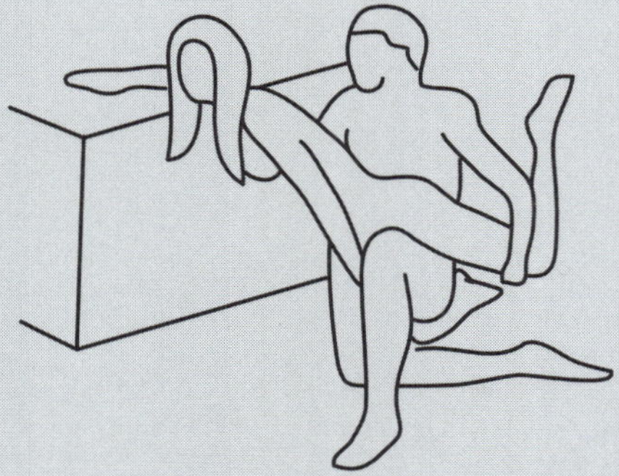

SO YOU LIKED THE LASAGNA . . .

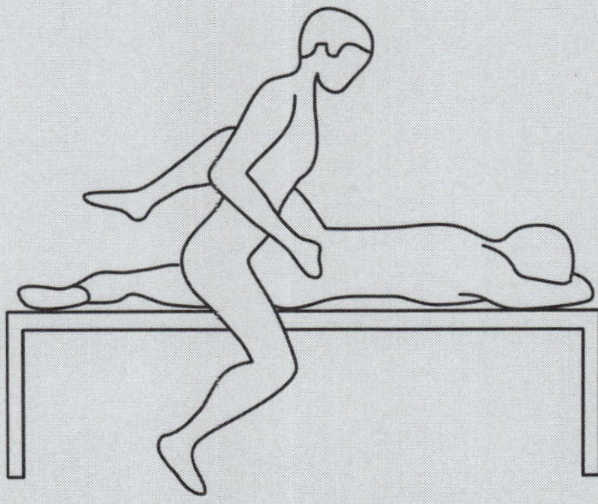

GRAB SOME BENCH

june.) 13

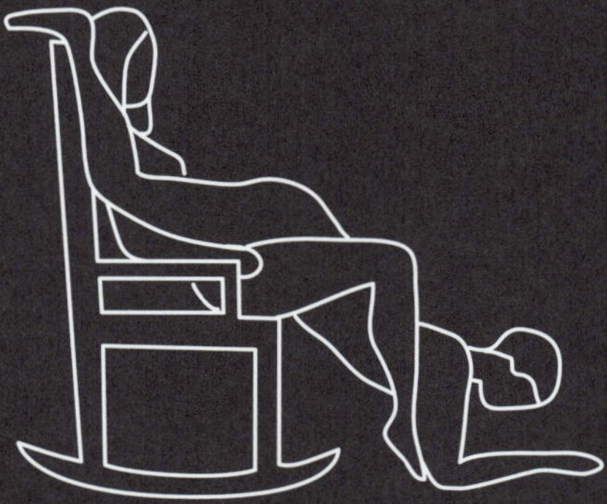

THE GLAZED TWIST

june.) 14

RAISING THE FLAG

june.)

15

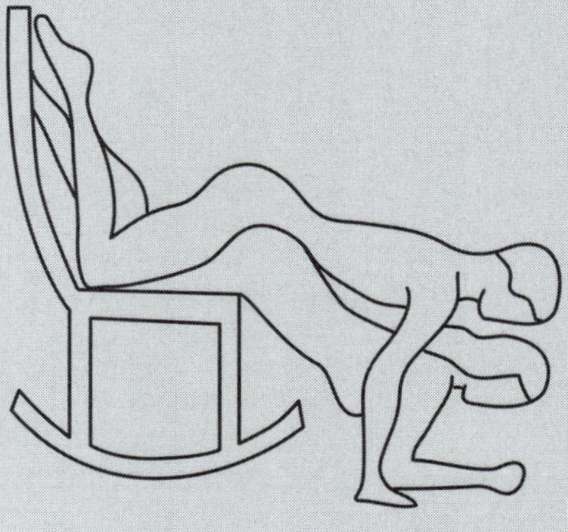

GETTIN' SLINKY

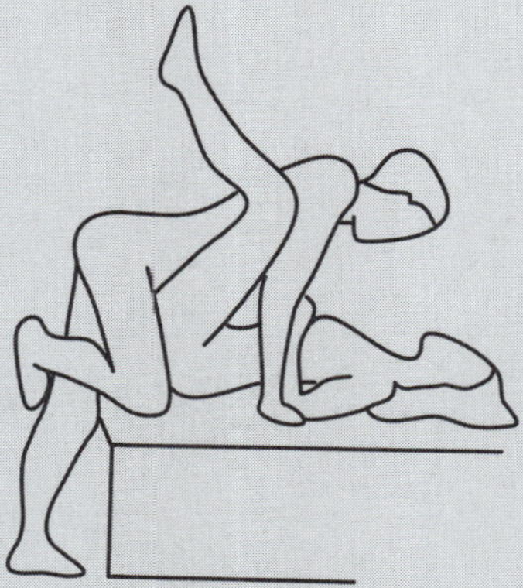

CLIMBING MOUNT PLEASANT

june.)

17

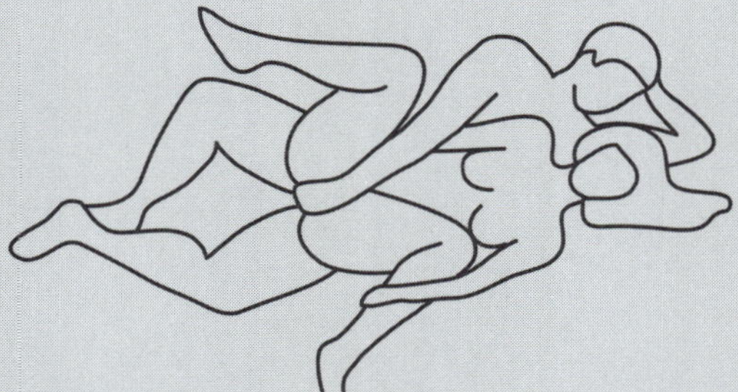

THE CHERRY PICKER

june.) **18**

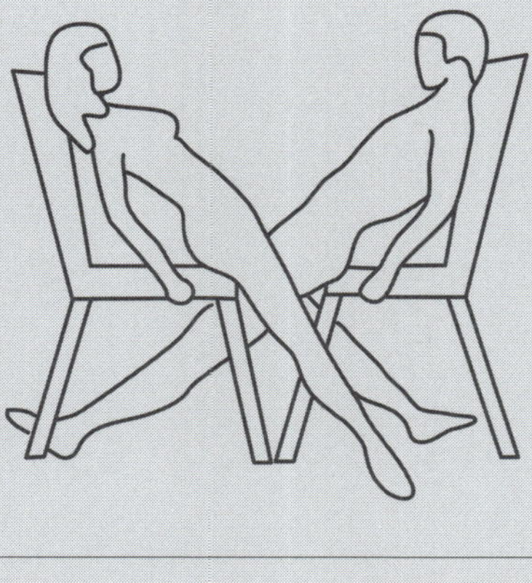

REGENERATION X

june.) **19**

THE RIGHT ANGLE

june.) **20**

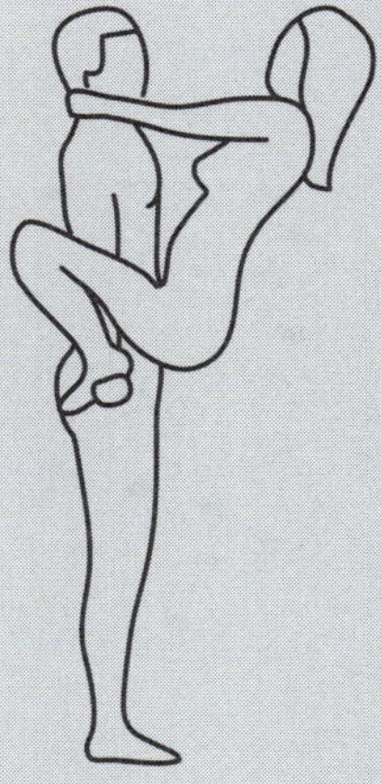

A-CUTE ANGLE

june.)

21

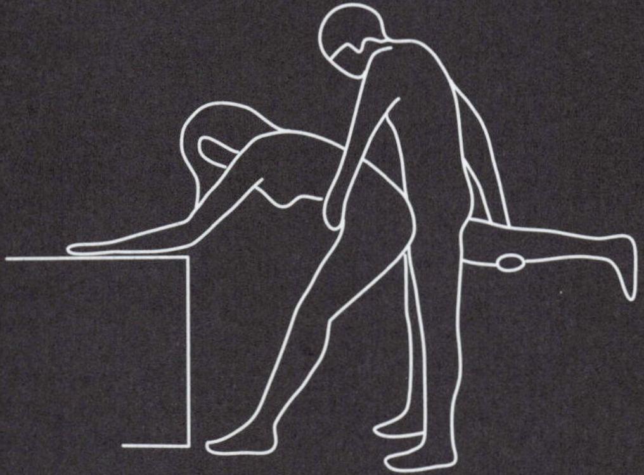

THE HURDLE

THE SUPER GLUE

june.) 23

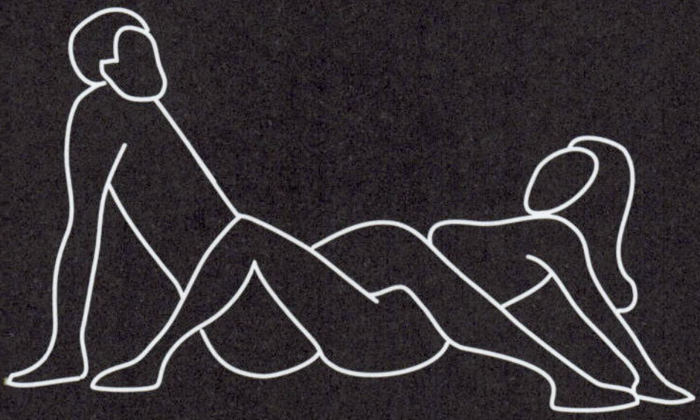

THE CRULLER

june.) **24**

THE SPRINGBOARD

june.) **25**

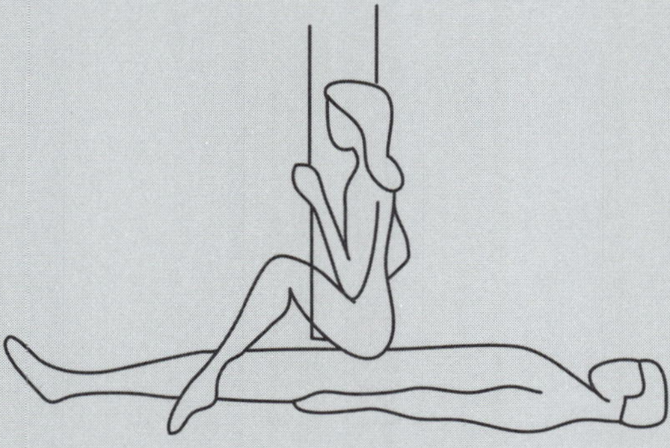

THE HAPPY LANDING

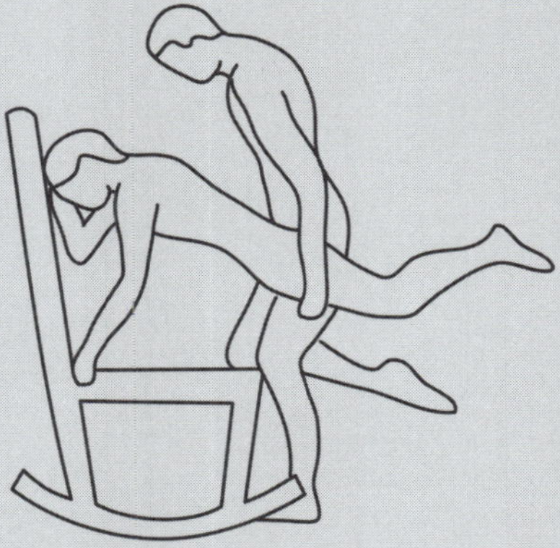

THE ROCK-HARD

june.)

27

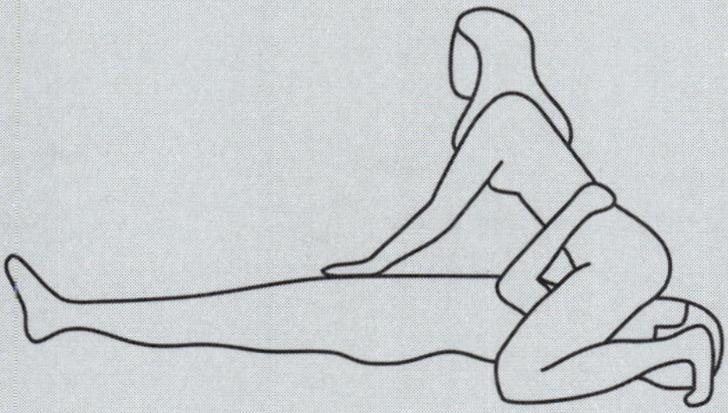

ON YOUR MARK!

june.)

28

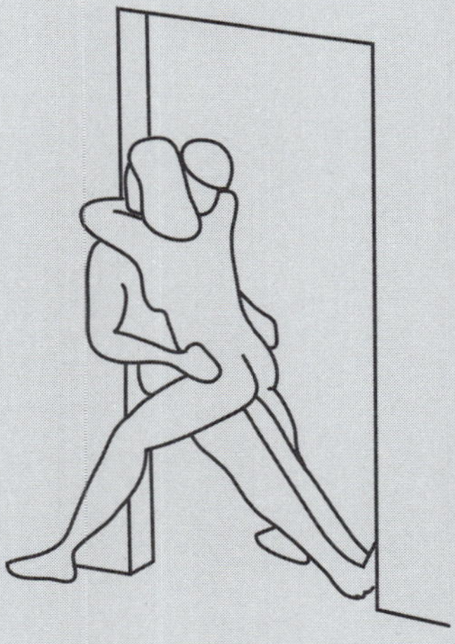

IMMORAL SUPPORT

june.) **29**

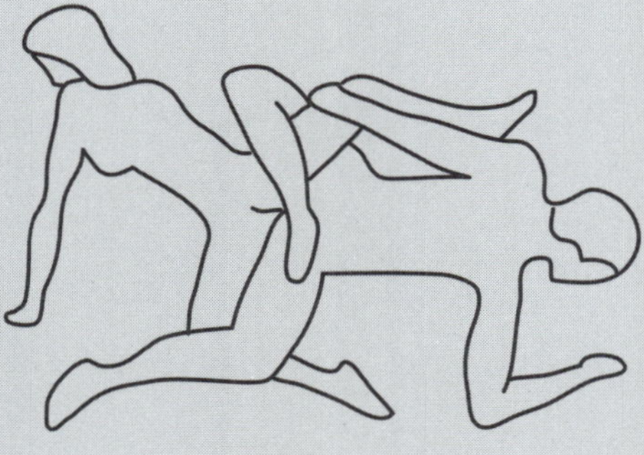

THE FIRE HYDRANT

june.) 30

THE REUNION

july.) 01

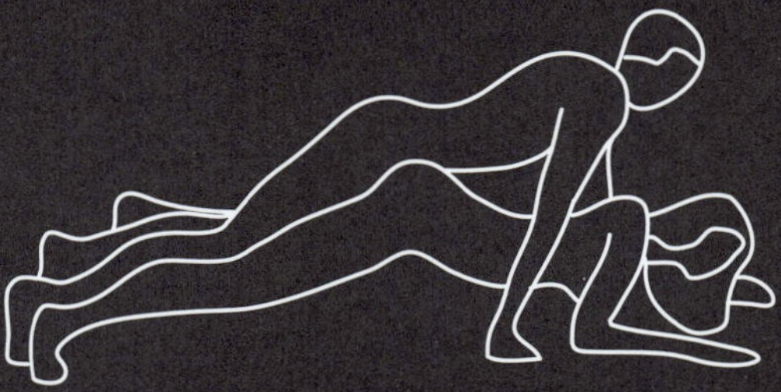

THE FLOW SESSION

july.) **02**

THE OXCART

july.) **03**

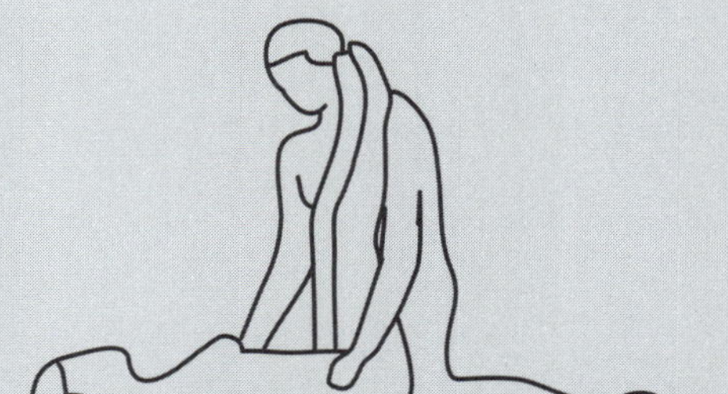

TO A "T"

july.) **04**

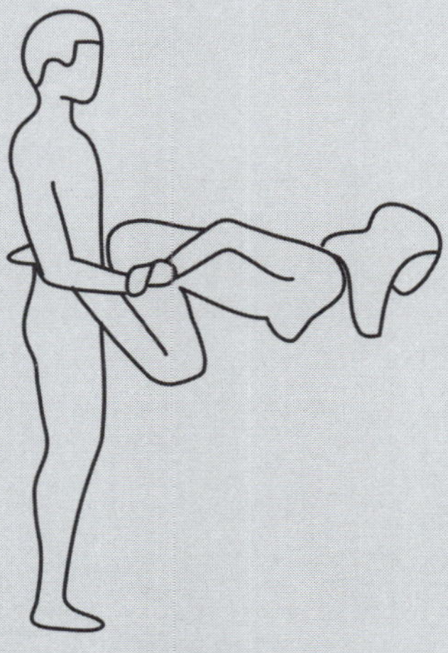

THE FIREWORKS

july.)

05

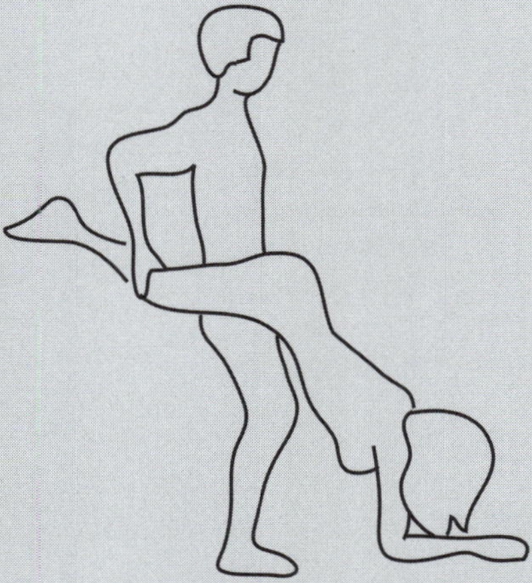

THE VACUUM

july.) **06**

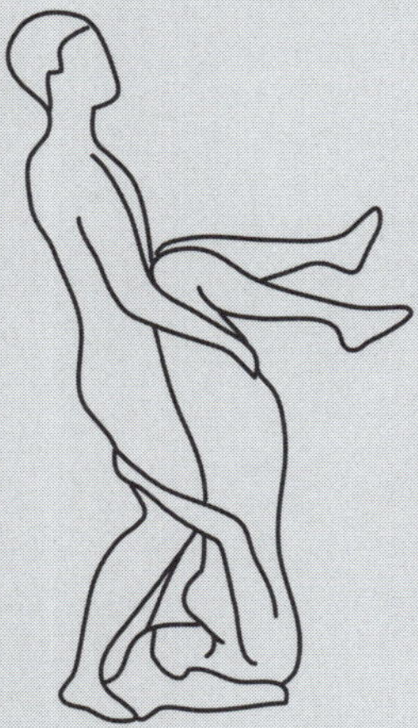

THE VIEW

july.)

07

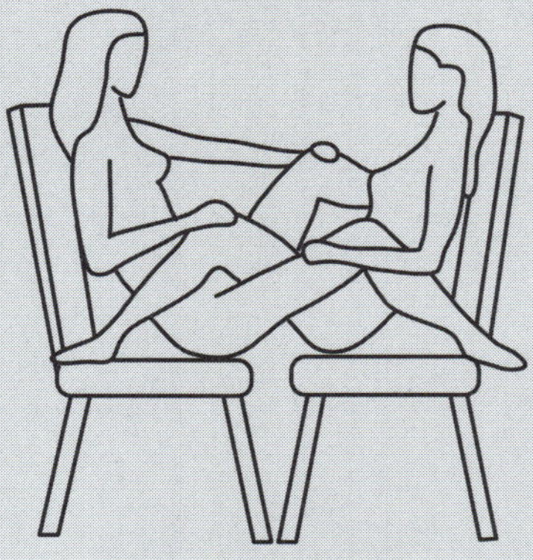

THE CAT'S CRADLE

july.) **08**

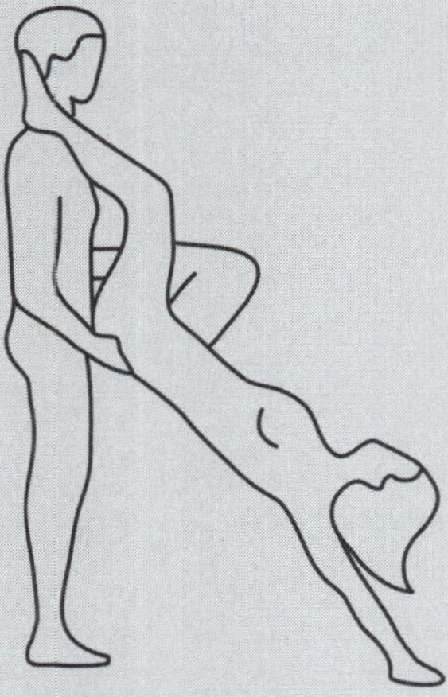

THE SUNDIAL

july.)

09

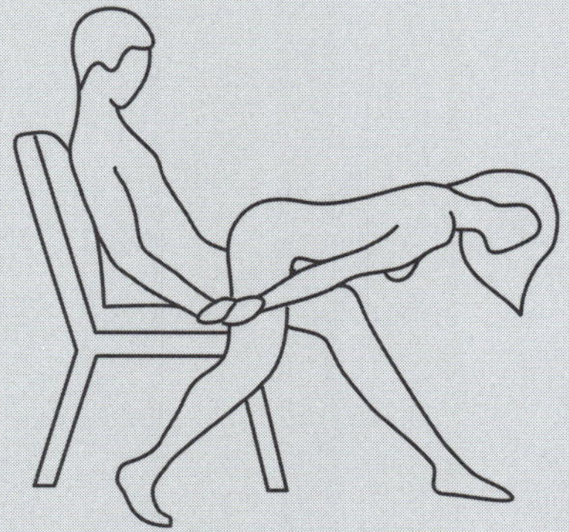

THE CRASH POSITION

july.) **10**

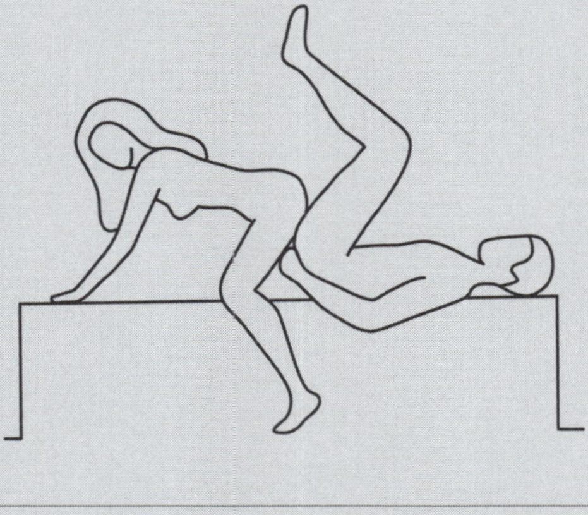

THE FIDGET SPINNER

july.)

11

ADDITION

july.) 12

THE ACCORDION

july.) 13

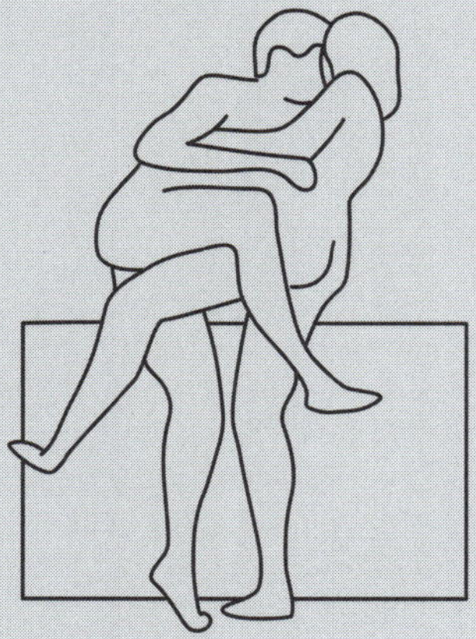

THE RIGHT HERE, RIGHT NOW

july.)

14

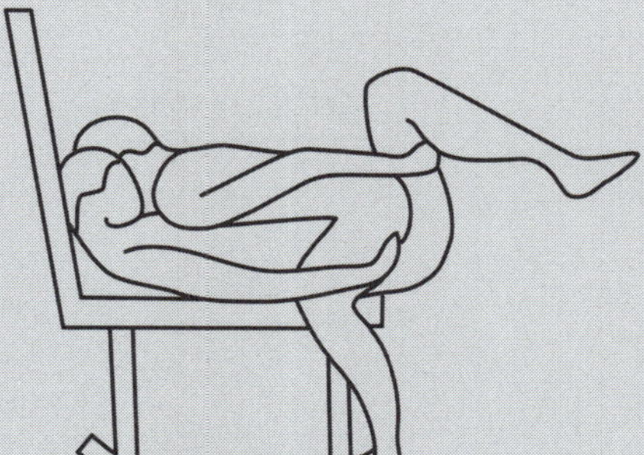

THE MAN-WICH

july.)

15

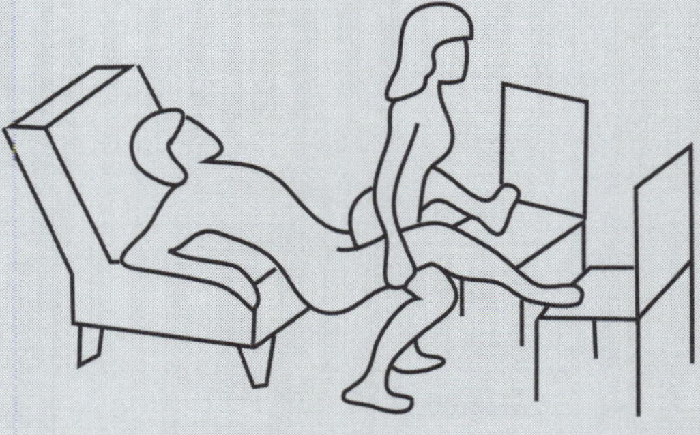

INTERIOR DECORATING

july.)

16

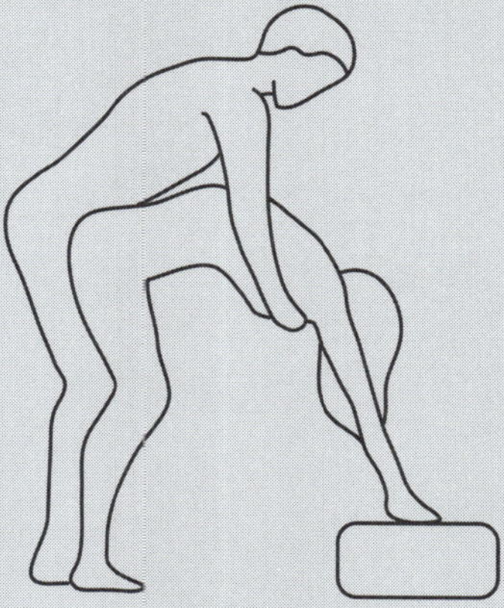

PARALLEL PLAY

july.)

17

GIVE ME A "U"

july.)

18

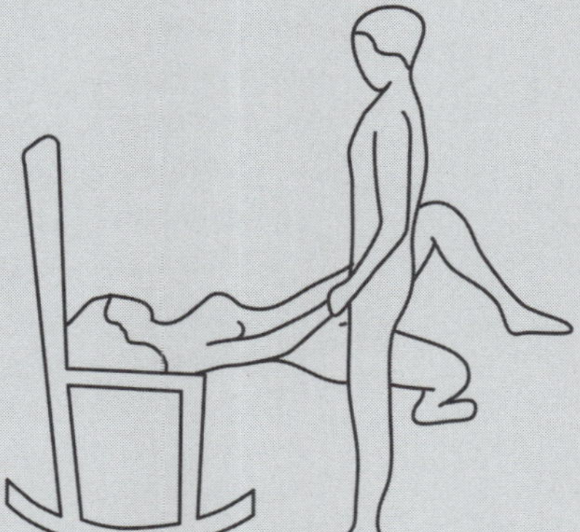

THE GRAPHIC AXIS

july.) 19

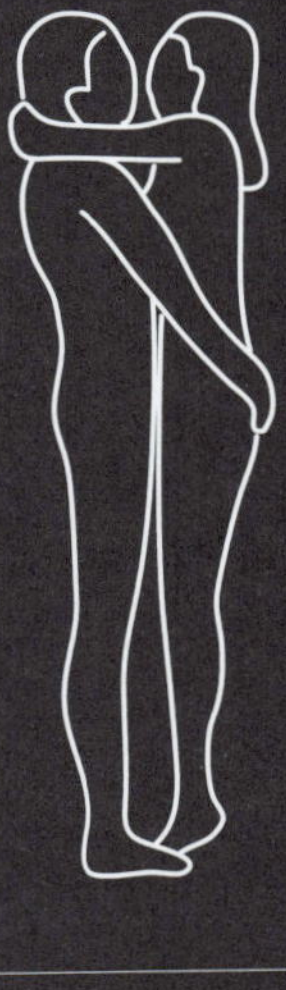

THE PRESSED SANDWICH

july.) 20

DEEP HEELING

july.) **21**

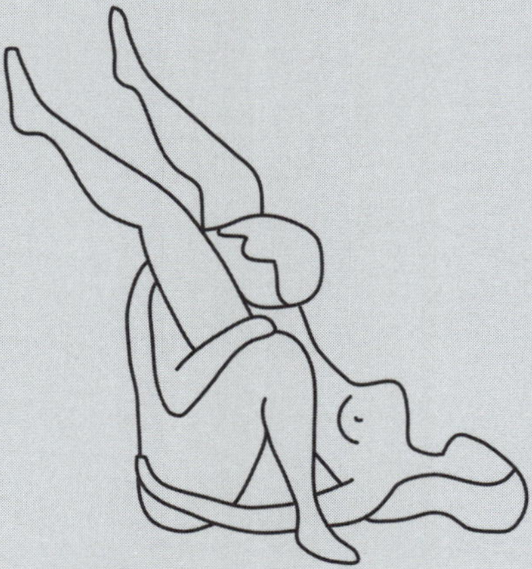

ALL UP IN THAT

july.) 22

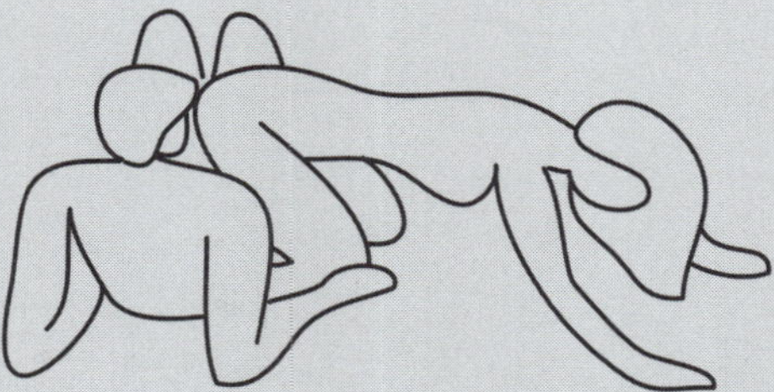

THE BUNNY HOP

july.)

23

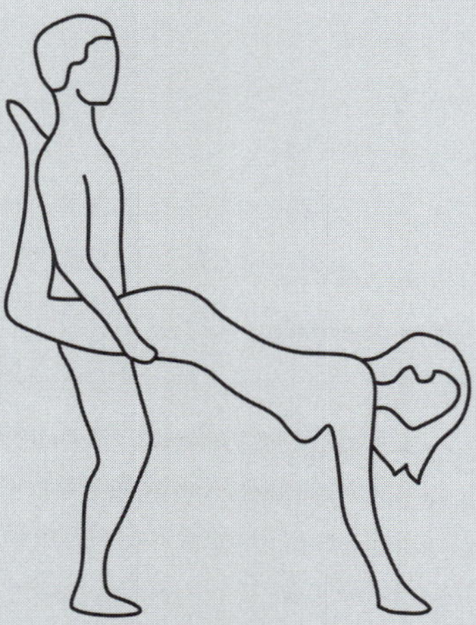

PUSH INS

july.) 24

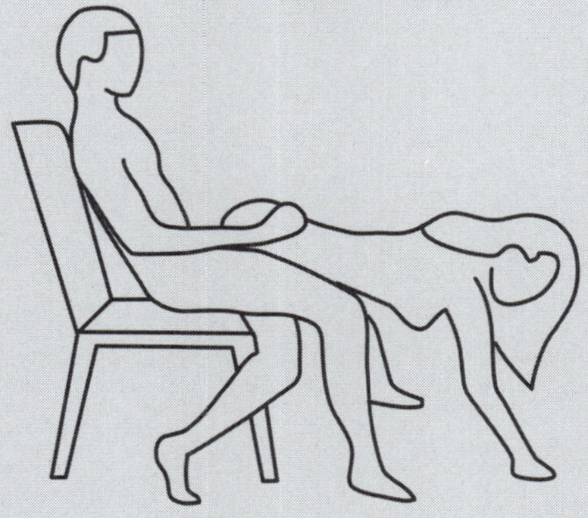

TV DINNER

july.)

25

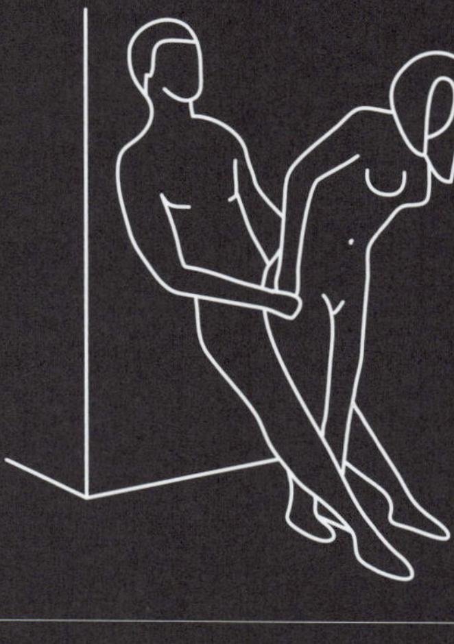

THE WEDGIE

july.) **26**

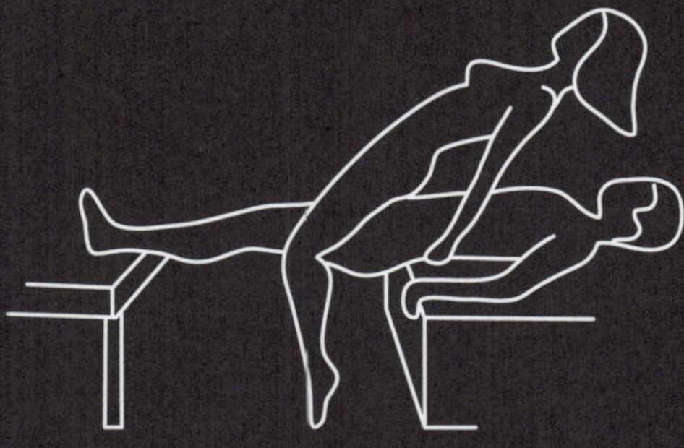

"IT'S CURVED . . ."

july.)

27

CHAIRWAY TO HEAVEN

july.) **28**

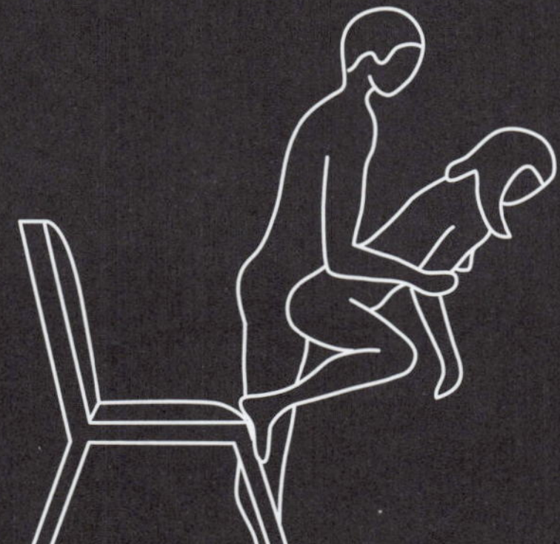

THE FALSE START

july.)

29

THE PRAYING MANTIS

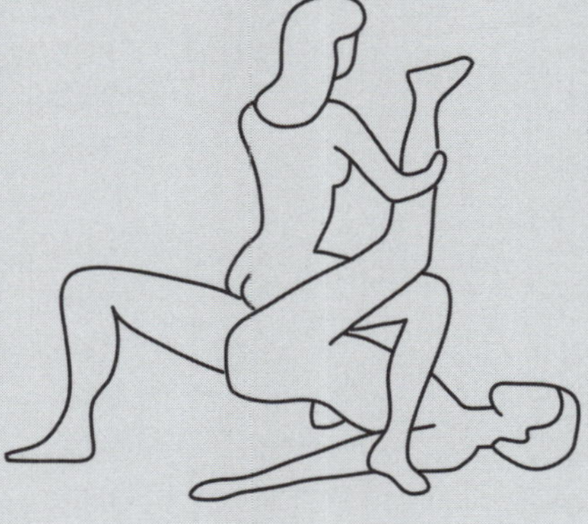

THE STICK SHIFT

july.)

31

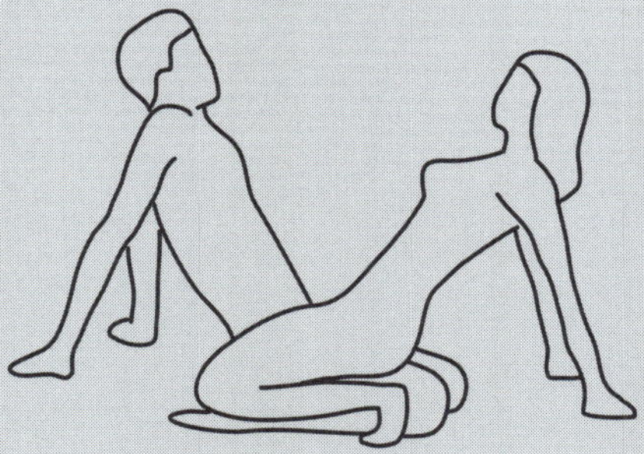

THE GRAND TETON

august.)

01

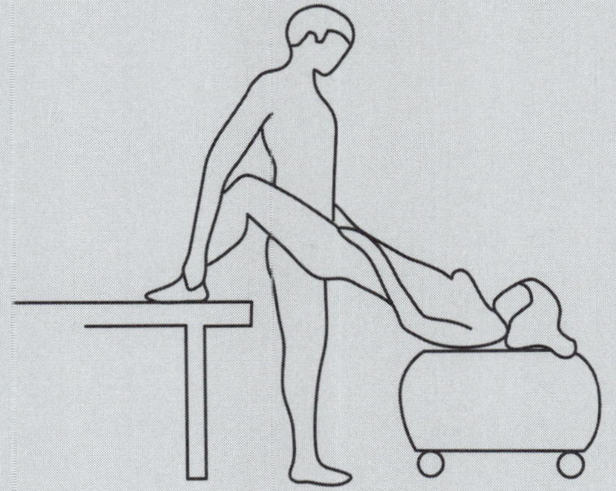

THE 4:30

august.) 02

THE BUTTERFLY CHAIR

august.) **03**

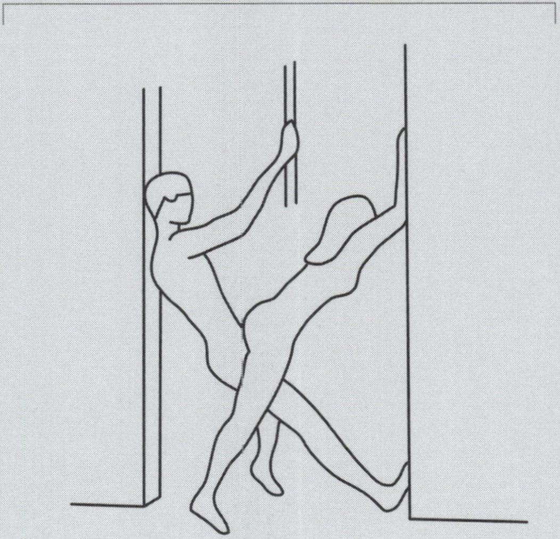

X MARKS THE SPOT

august.) 04

THE BUTTERCUP

august.) **05**

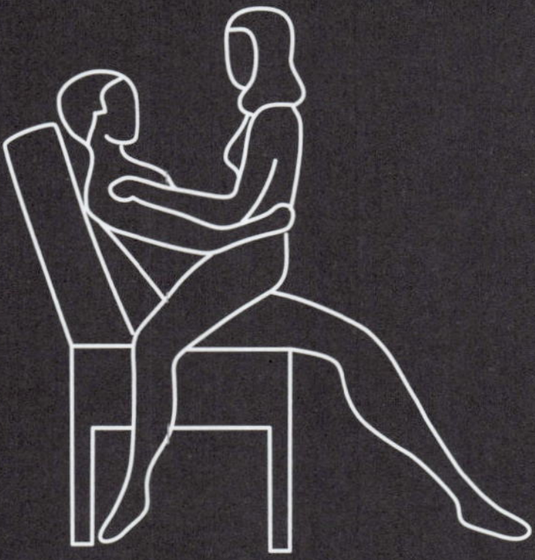

THE HOT SEAT

august.) **06**

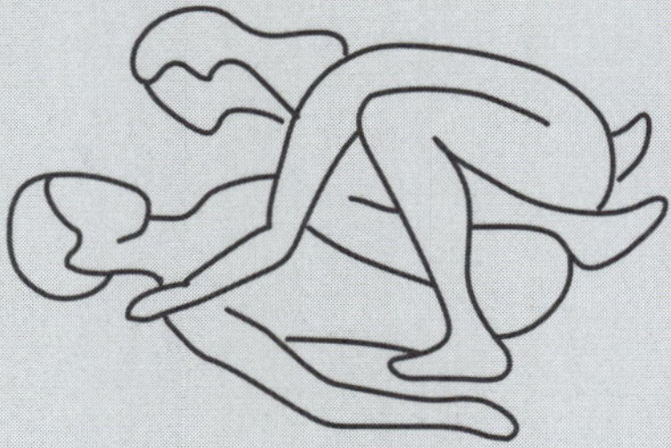

THE BREAKFAST BISCUIT

august.)

07

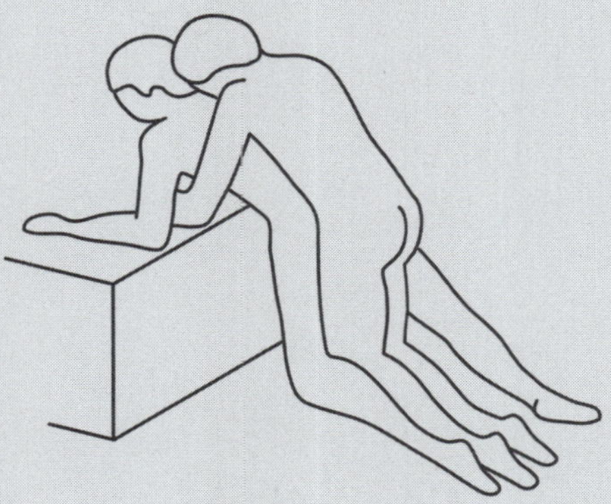

THE WET BLANKET

august.)

08

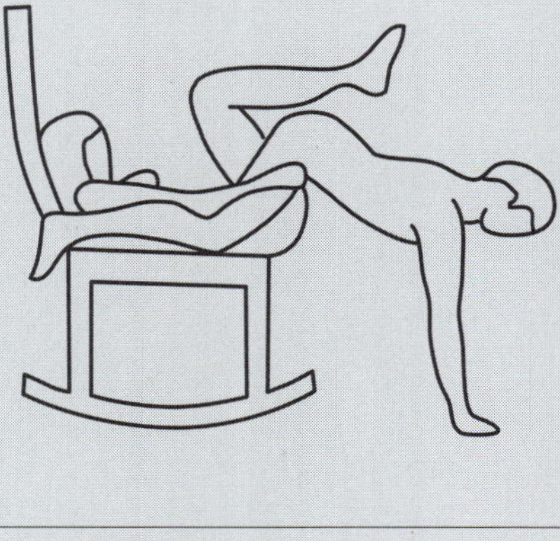

A ROCKING GOOD TIME

august.) 09

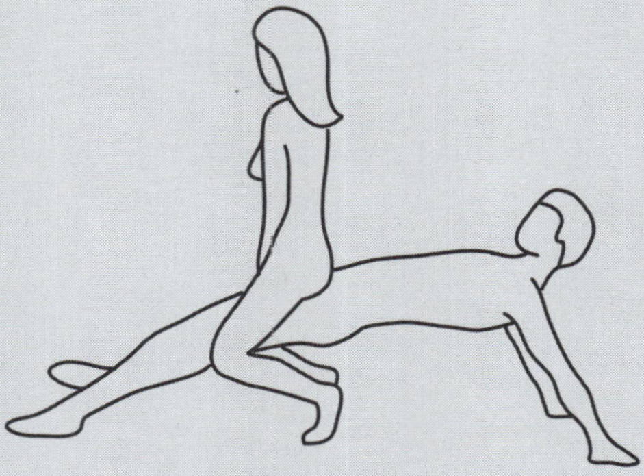

SLIDING DOWN THE BANISTER

august.)

10

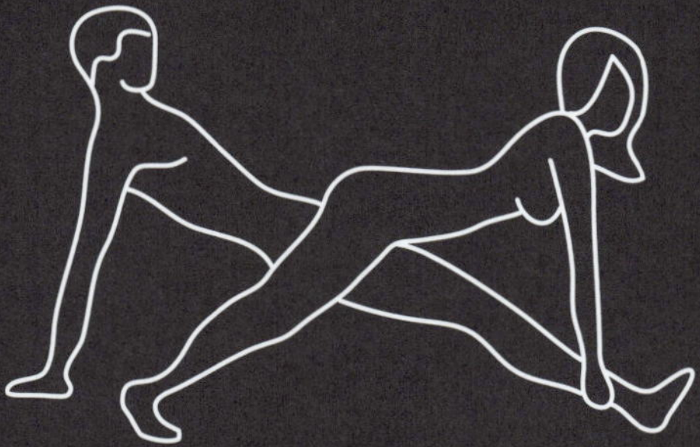

THE WARM-UP STRETCH

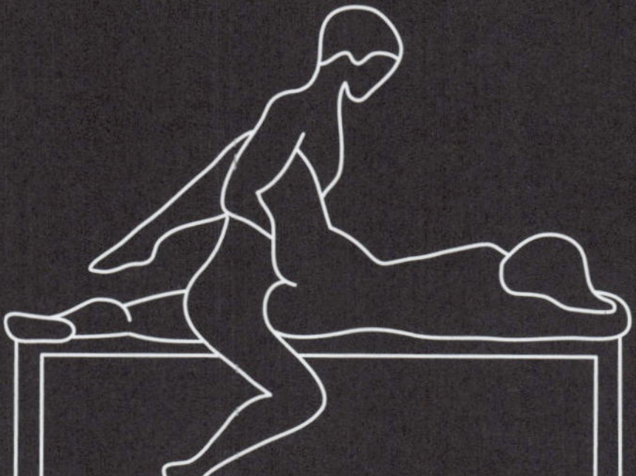

THREADING THE NEEDLE

august.)

12

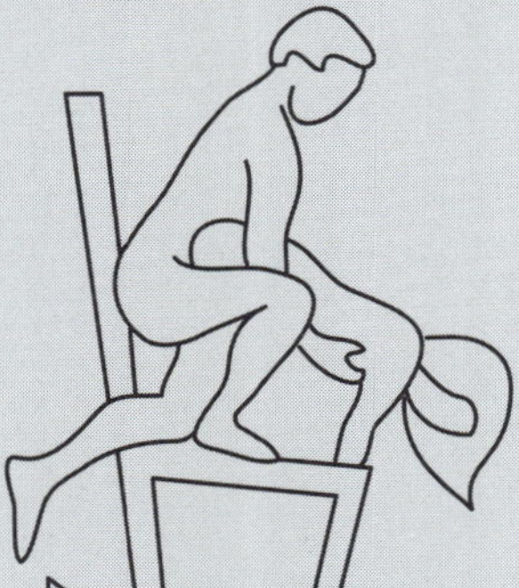

BANGING IN THE BALANCE

august.) 13

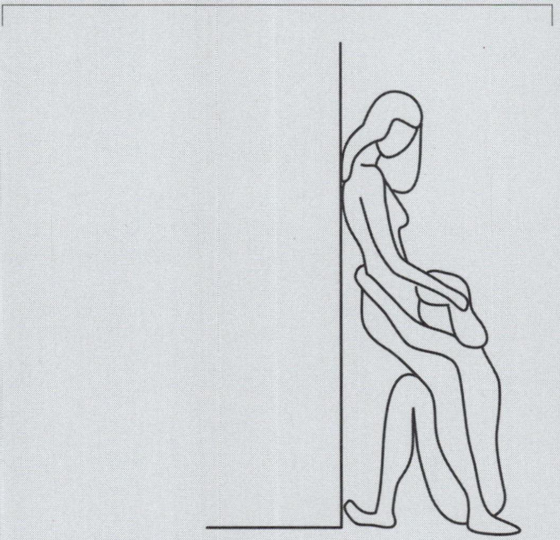

SNORKELING

august.) 14

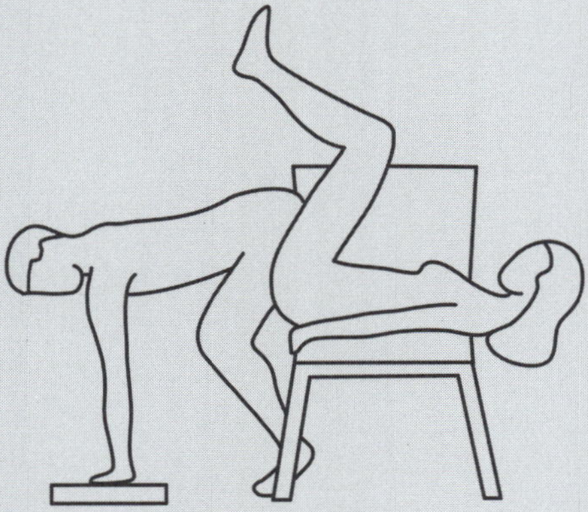

CHEEKY GREETINGS

august.)

15

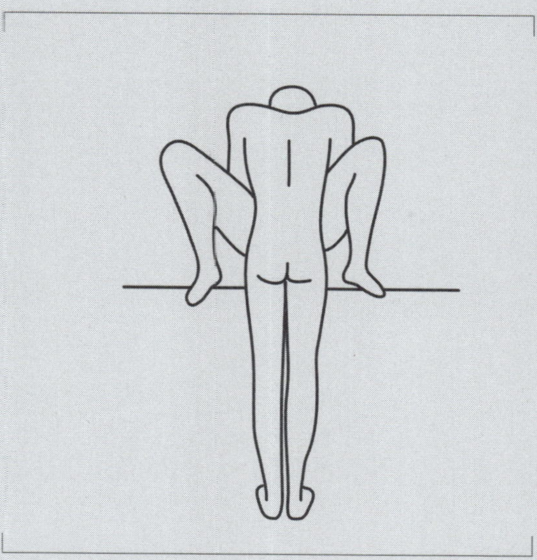

OVER THE COUNTER

august.)

16

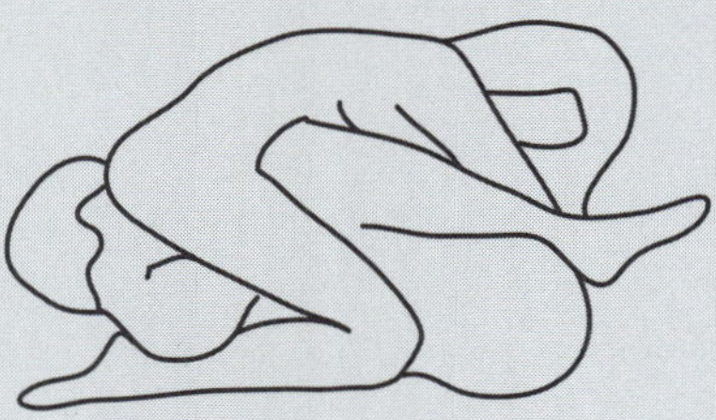

MY ROCK

august.) **17**

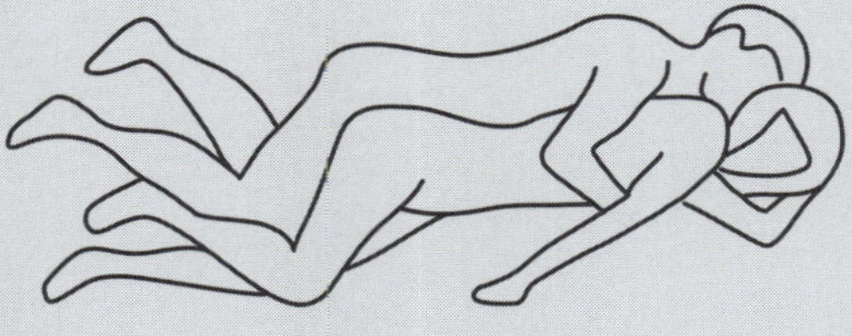

THE GREASY SPOON

august.) 18

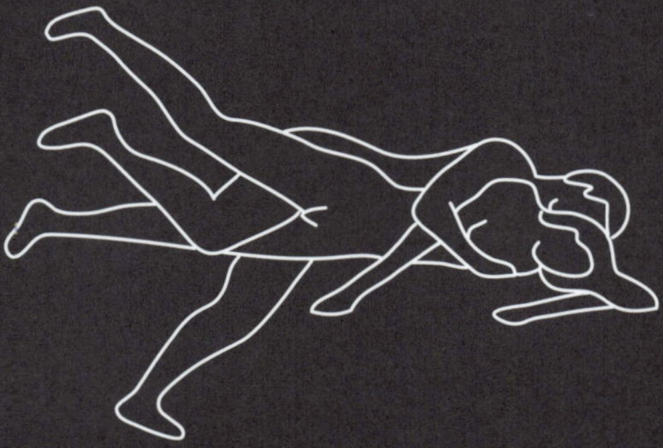

THE SQUID

august.) **19**

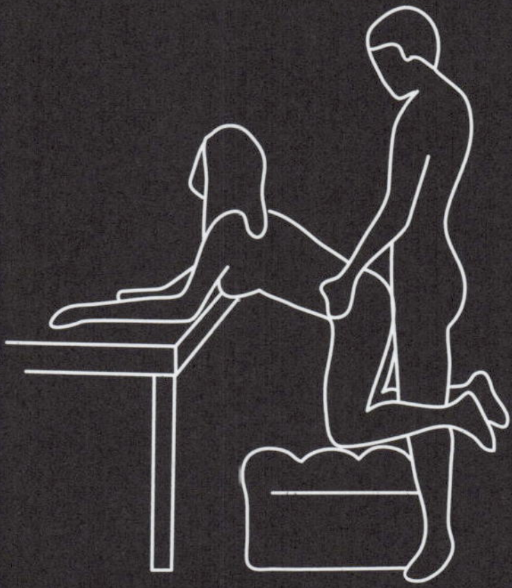

THE OTTOMAN BOTTOMMAN

august.) **20**

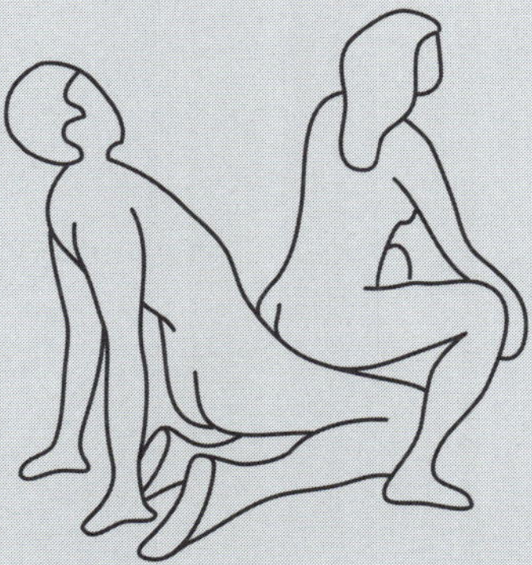

PAY IT FORWARD

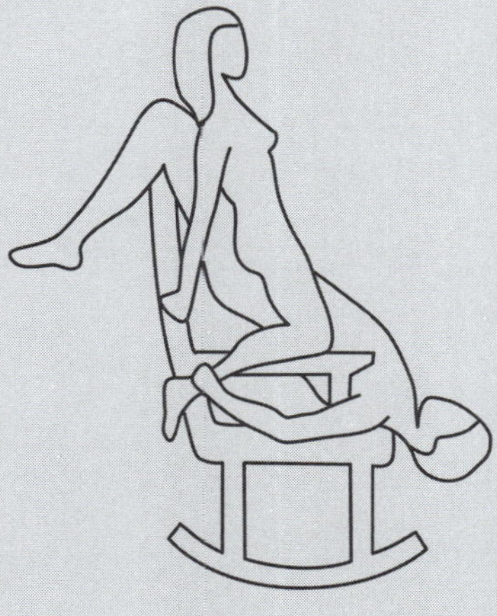

SO WRONG IT'S RIGHT

august.)

22

THE HOLD STEADY

august.)

23

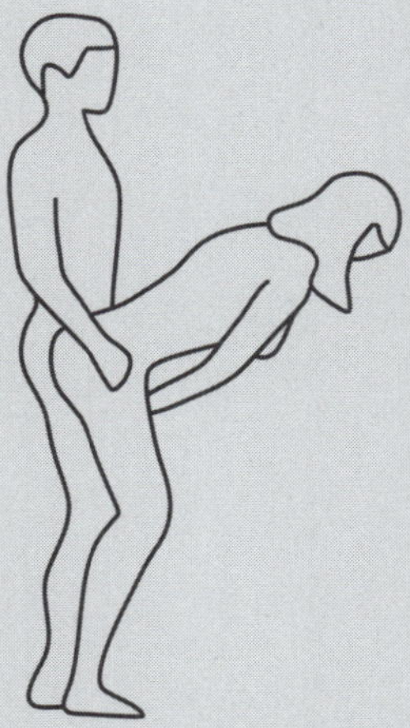

THE LOST KEY

august.)

24

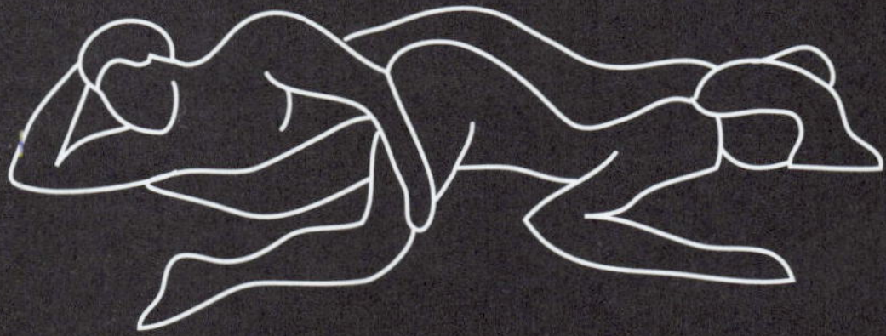

THE THINKER

august.) **25**

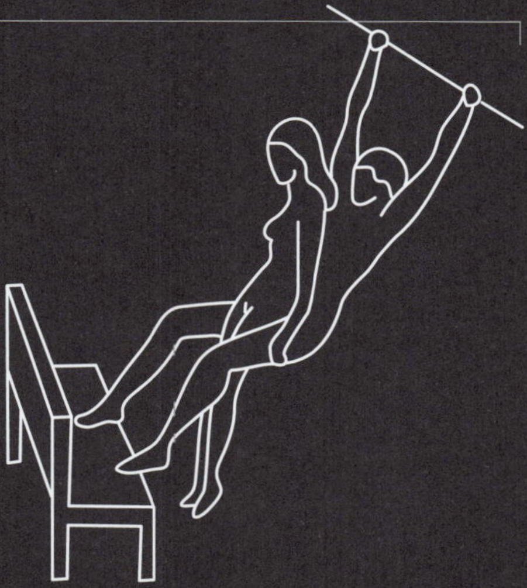

THE FULL SWING

august.)

26

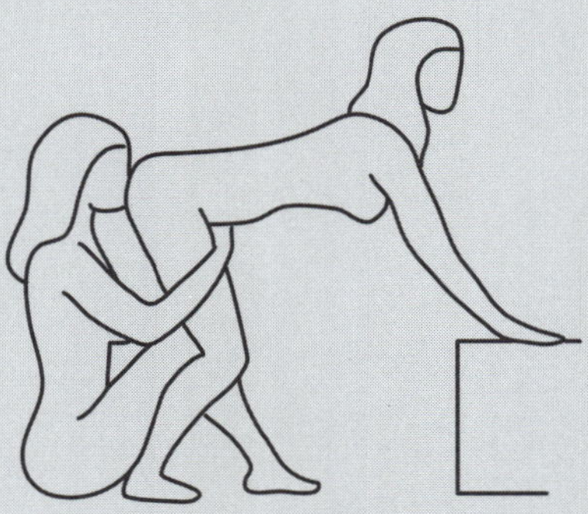

THE THERMOMETER

august.) **27**

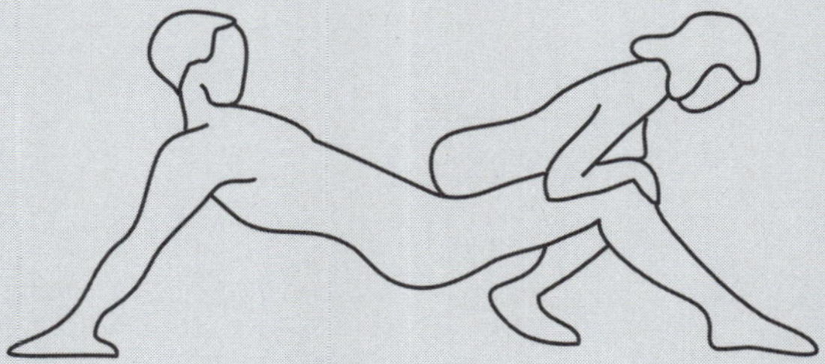

DOWN IN FRONT!

august.)

28

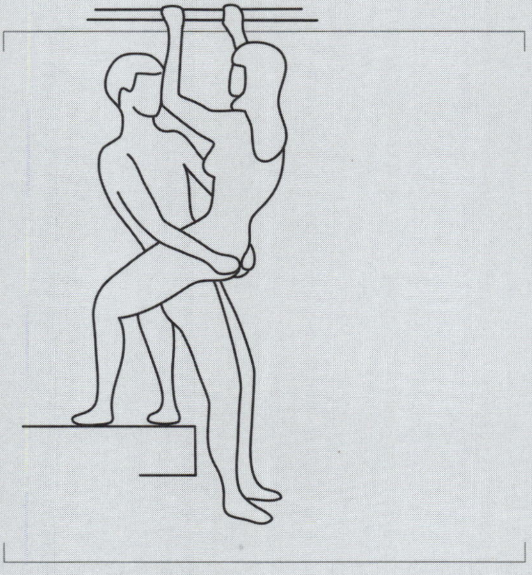

THE HOLD ON

august.) **29**

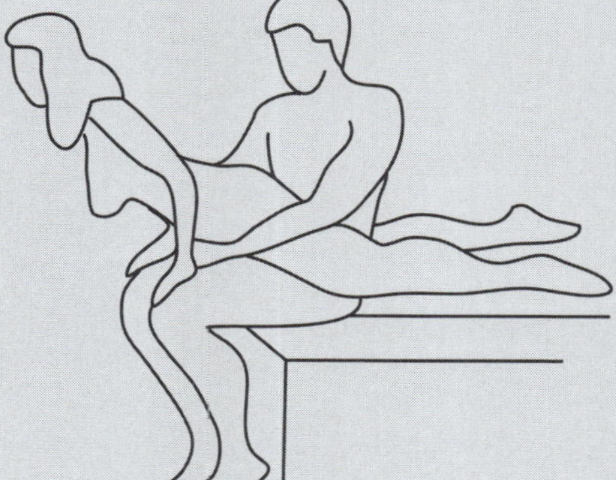

THE GARGOYLE

august.) 30

THE OYSTER, MY WORLD

august.)

31

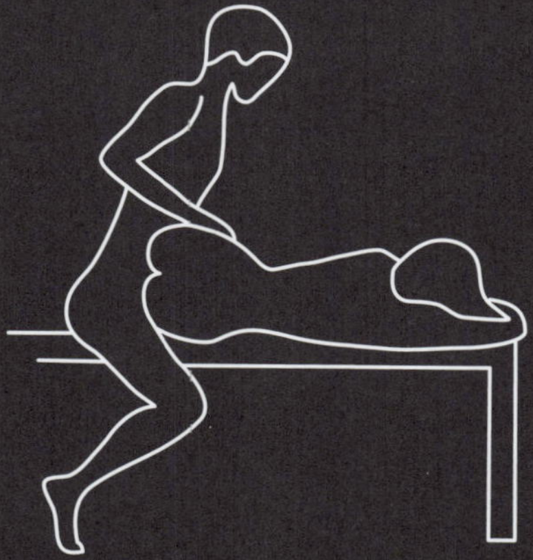

THE INTERSECTION

september.)

01

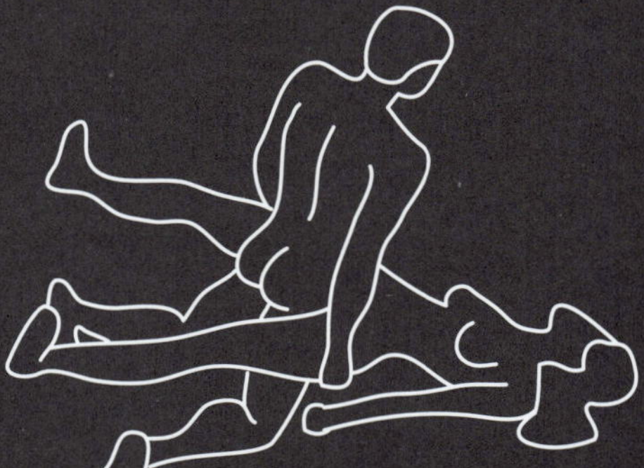

THE DOWSING ROD

september.)

02

THE LEG UP

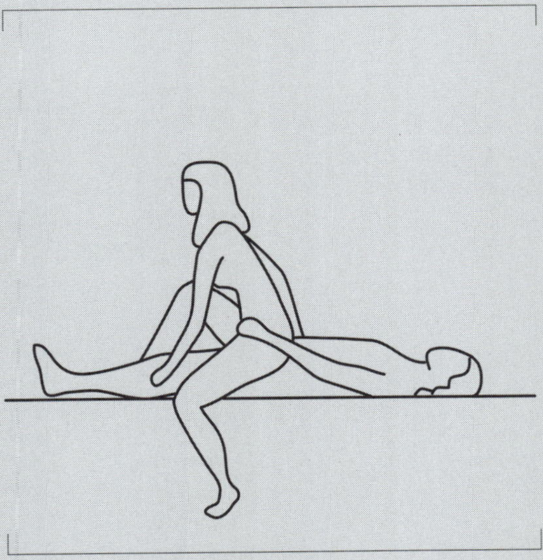

HOPPING THE FENCE

september.)

04

SLIDING INTO HOME

september.)

05

THE HANG LOW

september.) **06**

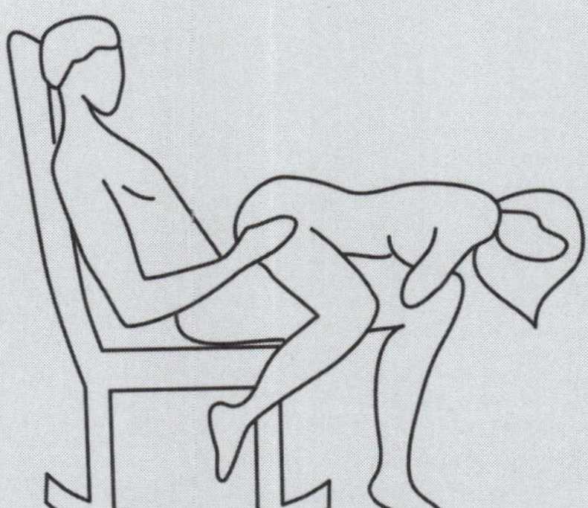

BACK IN THE SADDLE

september.)

07

THE TUGBOAT

september.)

08

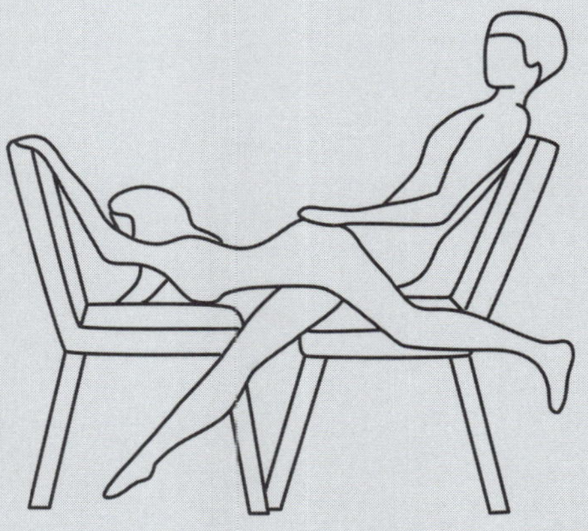

THE LAPTOP

september.) **09**

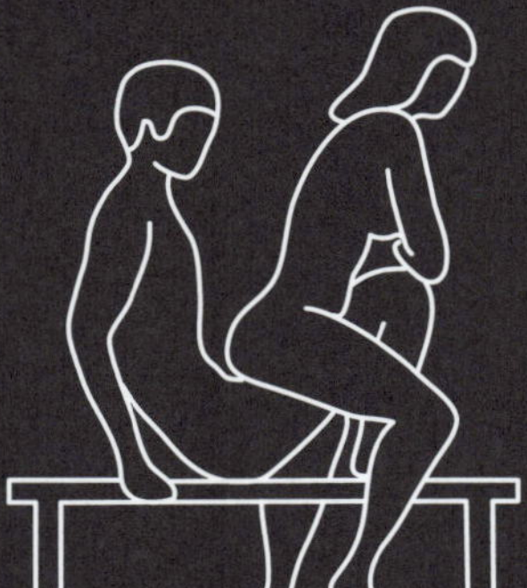

THE KNEE DEEP

september.)

10

THE ONSCREEN KISS

september.)

11

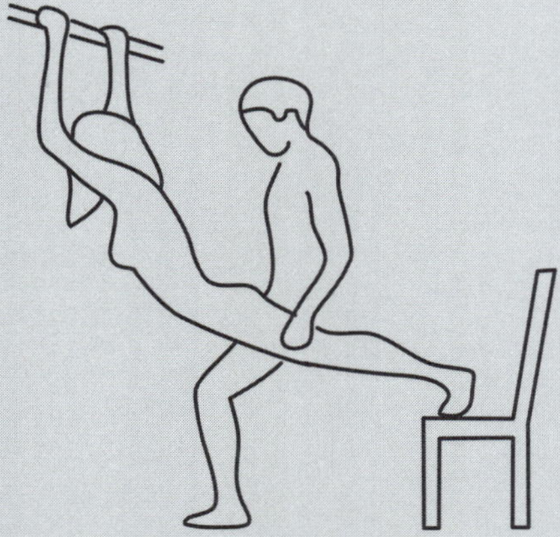

BANG-GLIDING

september.) **12**

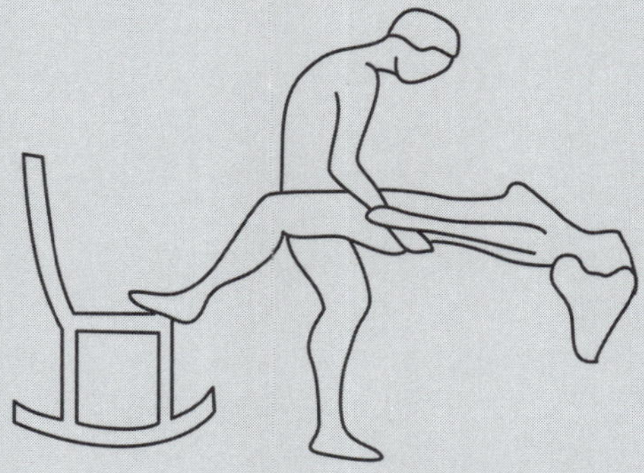

GET OFF YOUR ROCKER

september.)

13

PULLING A FAST ONE

september.) **14**

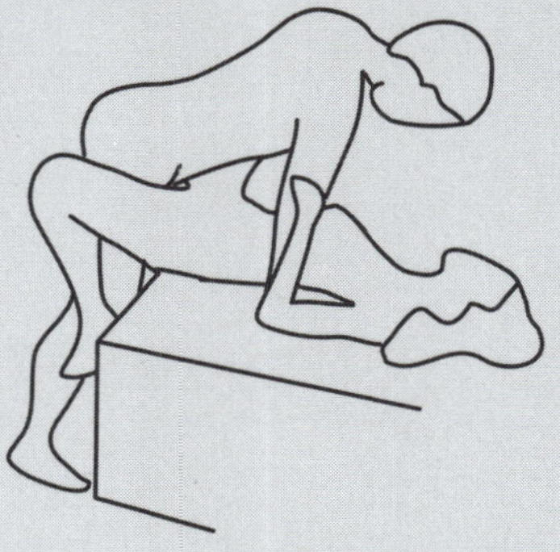

LOVE ON TOP

september.) **15**

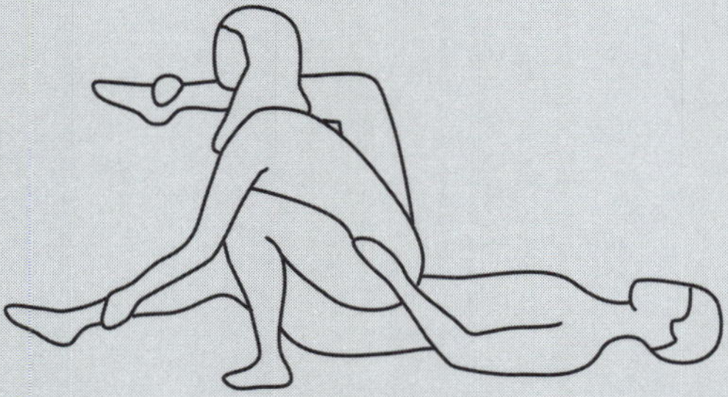

THE PEDICURE

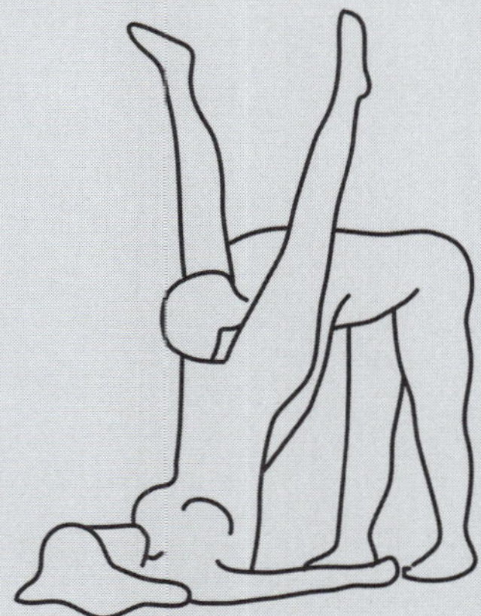

THE DEEP DIVE

september.) 17

FEELING THE BURN

september.) **18**

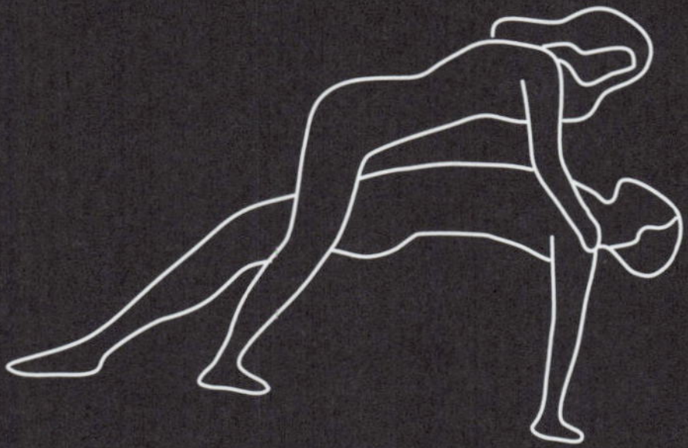

THE WILDCAT

september.) 19

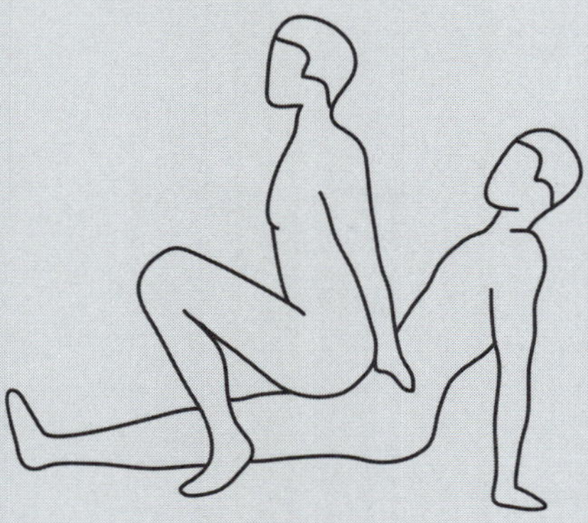

THE LAY-Z-BOYS

september.)

20

THE TÊTE-À-TÊTE

september.) **21**

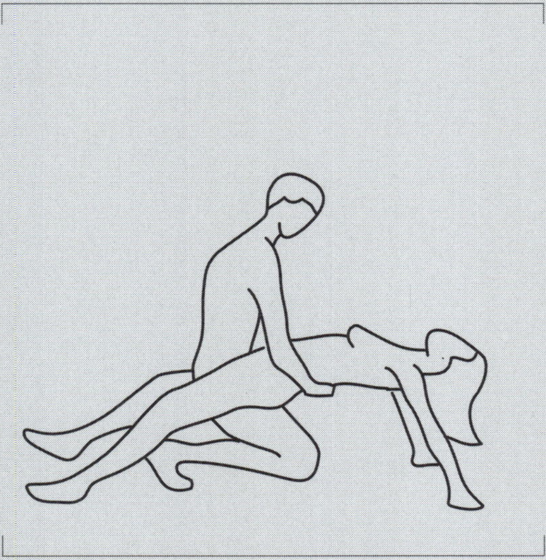

THE LOUNGE CHAIR

september.)

22

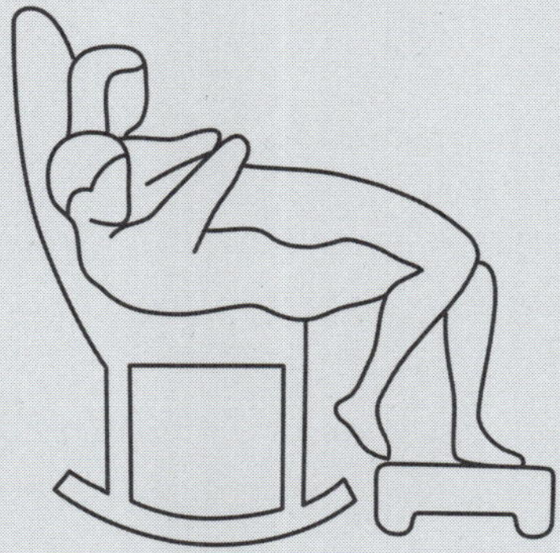

STUBBORNNESS

september.) 23

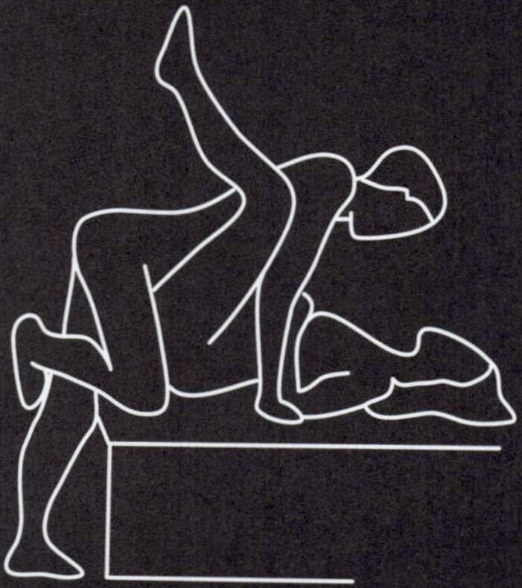

THE BIKE PUMP

september.)

24

THE SHOWER CURTAIN

september.) 25

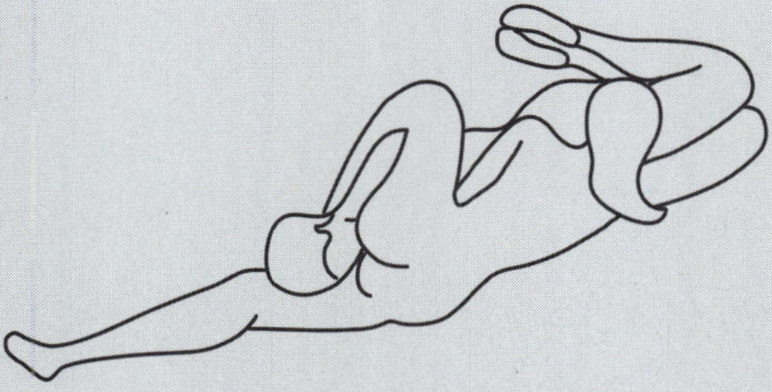

THE CARTESIAN CIRCLE

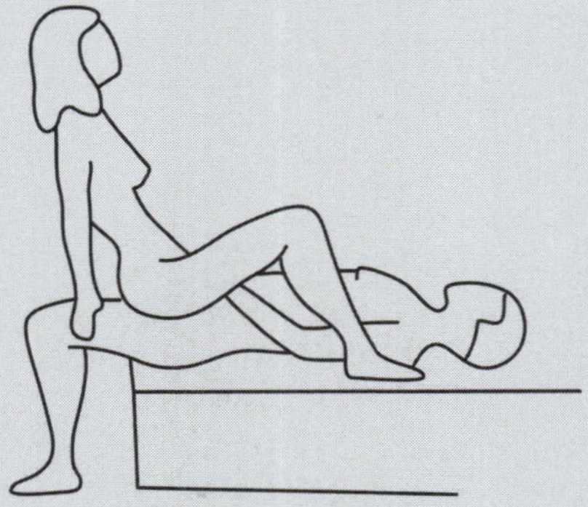

THE LEAN BACK

september.)

27

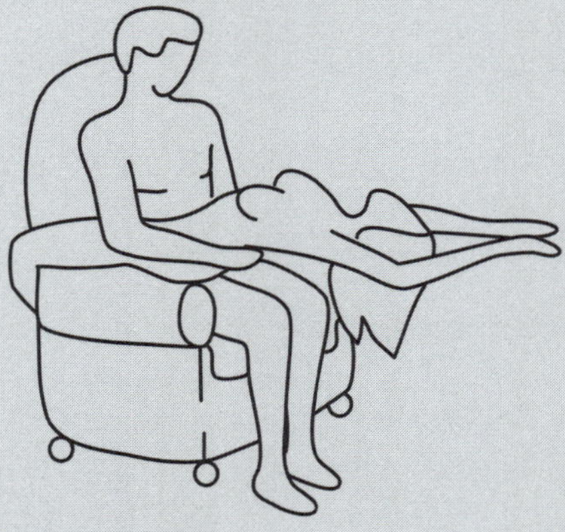

THE REMOTE CONTROL

september.)

28

A SEAT AT THE TABLE

september.)

29

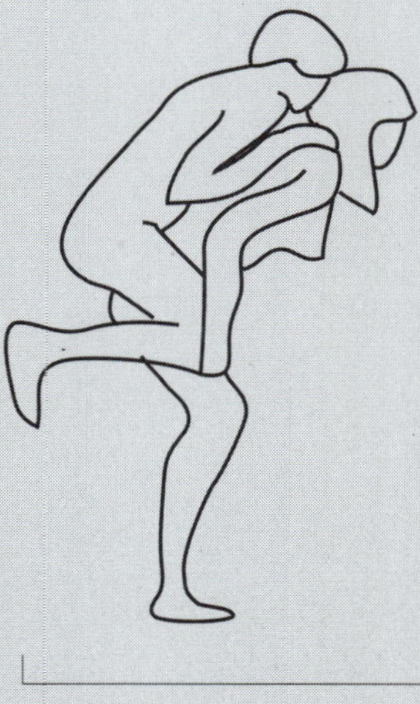

THE PIGGYBACK

september.)

30

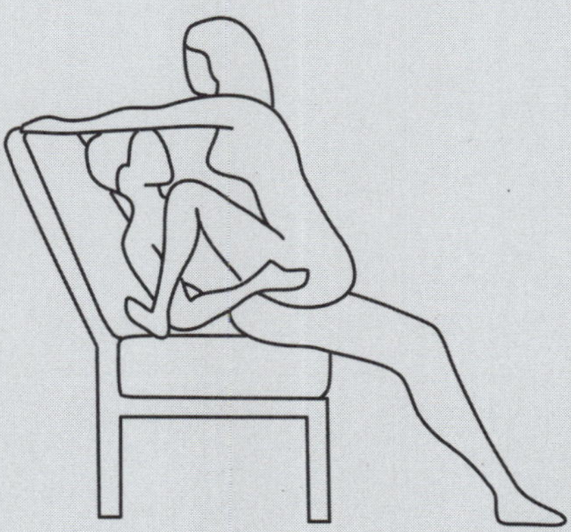

THE COXSWAIN

october.) **01**

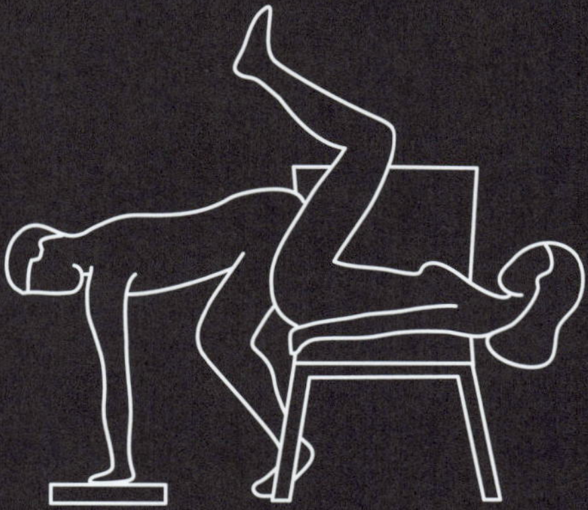

THE AWKWARD MOMENT

october.) **02**

THE VENN DIAGRAM

october.) 03

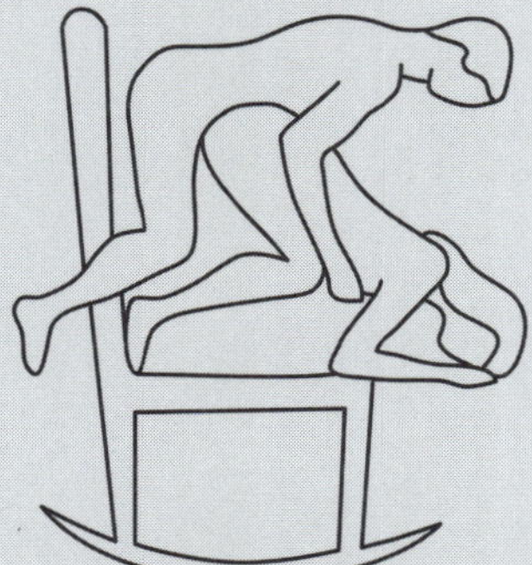

THE THRILL RIDE

BETWEEN A ROCKER AND A HARD PLACE

october.) **05**

THE T-BONE

october.)

06

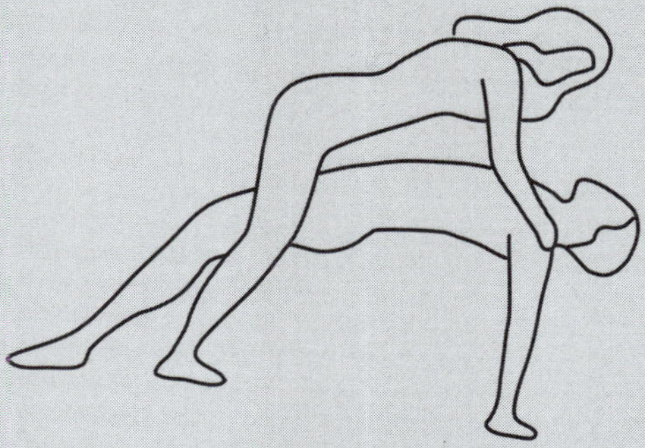

THE TREASURE CHEST

october.) 07

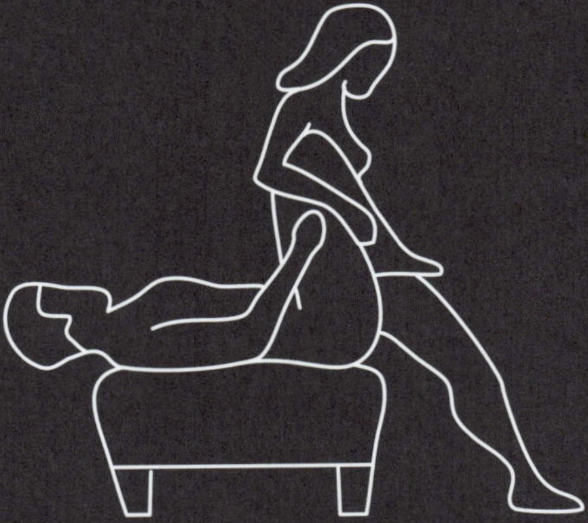

THE LEAN-TO

october.) 08

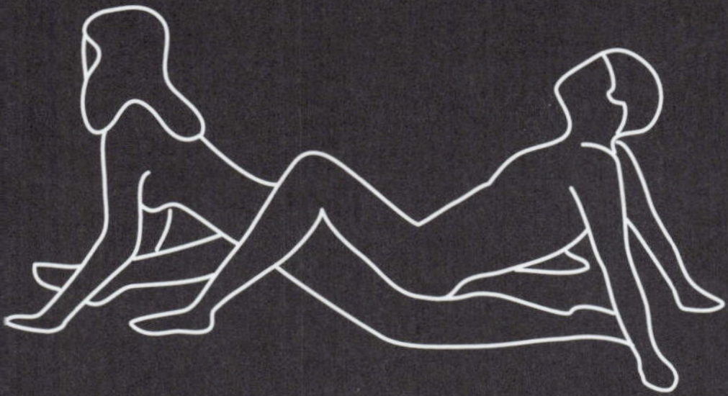

THE LONDON BRIDGE

october.) 09

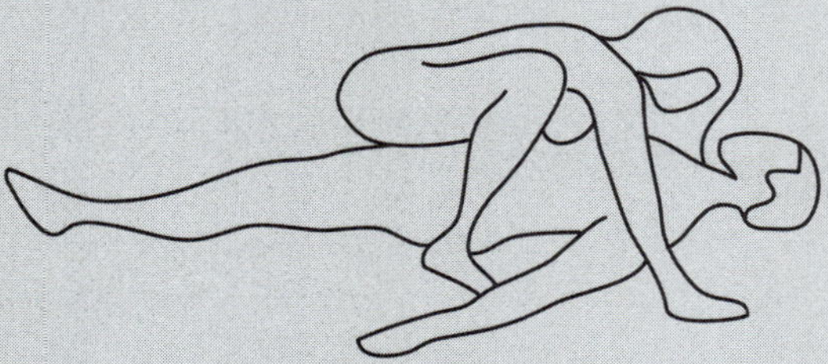

THE HEARTBURN

october.) **10**

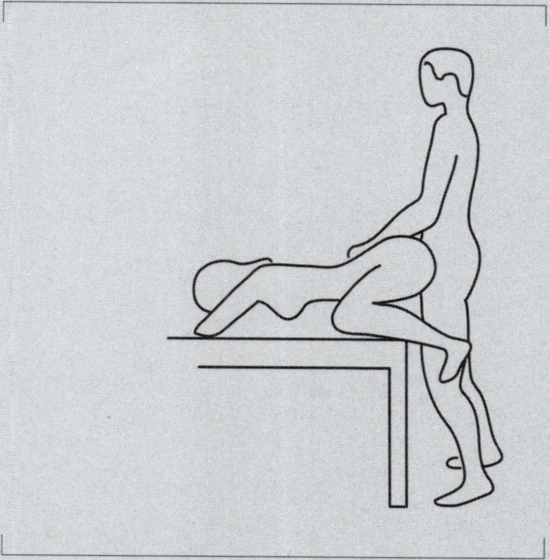

THE CENTERPIECE

october.) 11

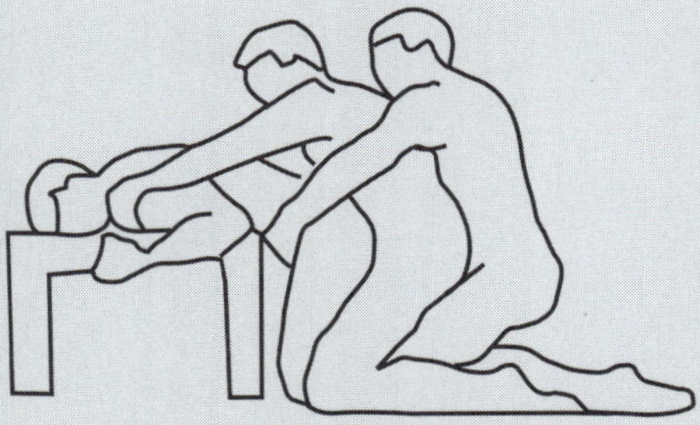

THE GROUP HUG

october.) **12**

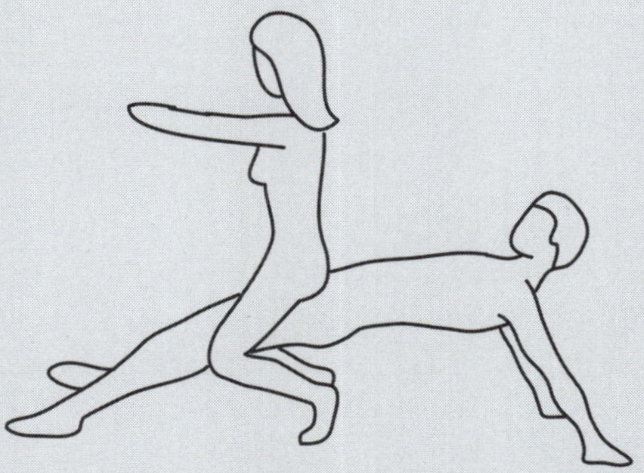

LAND HO!

october.) **13**

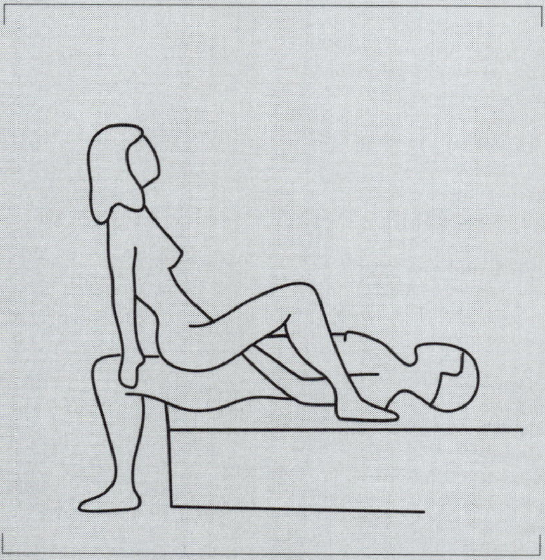

SITTING PRETTY

october.)

14

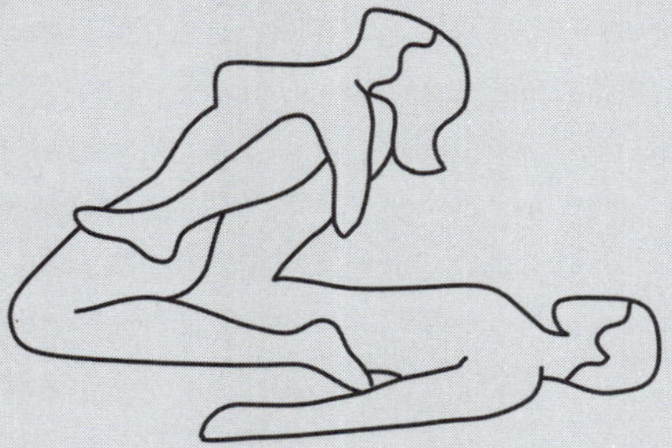

THE REALIGNMENT

october.) 15

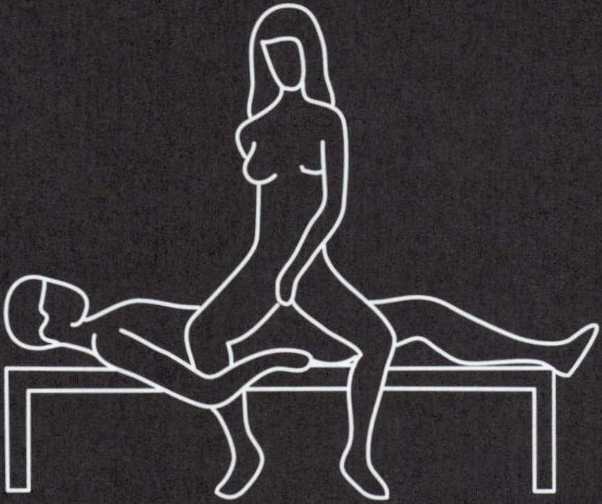

THE COASTER

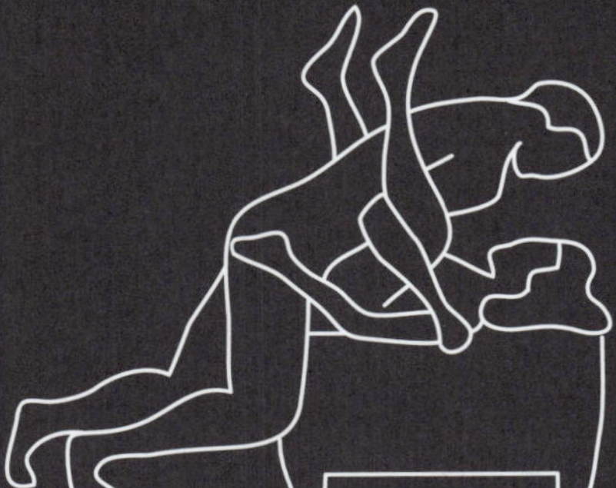

REARRANGING THE FURNITURE

october.) **17**

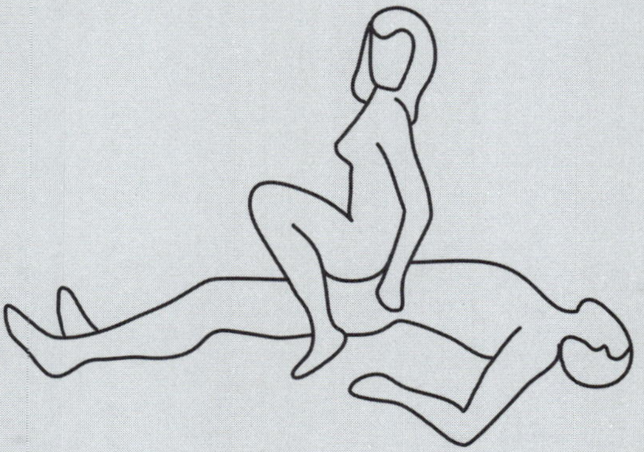

SELF-SERVICE

october.)

18

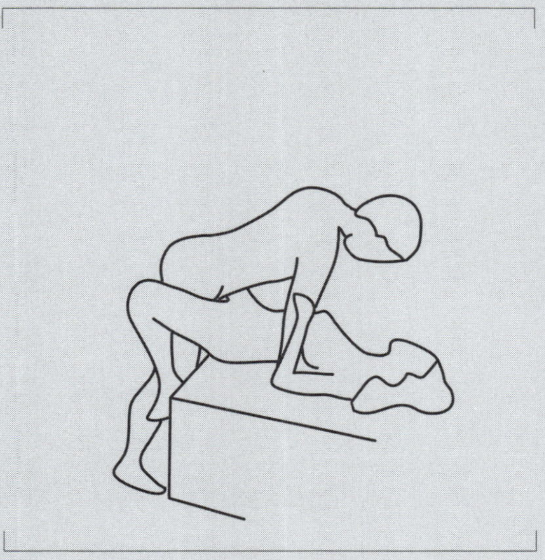

COUNTER SERVICE

october.) **19**

THE LOST CONTACT

THE PAPER CLIP

october.)

21

A FLYING F*CK

october.) 22

THE VITRUVIAN

october.) 23

THE LUMBERJACKS

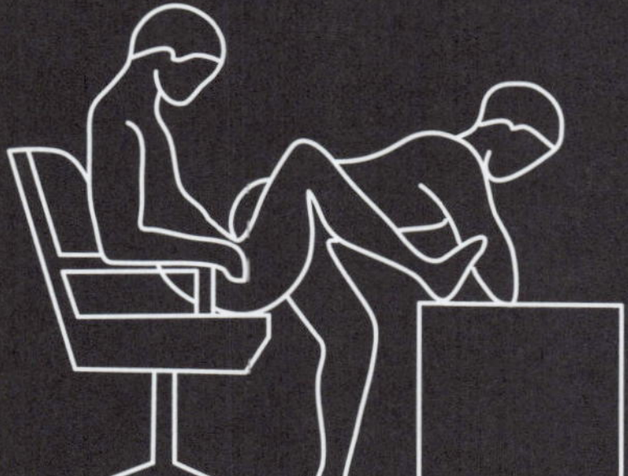

ON A ROLL

october.) 25

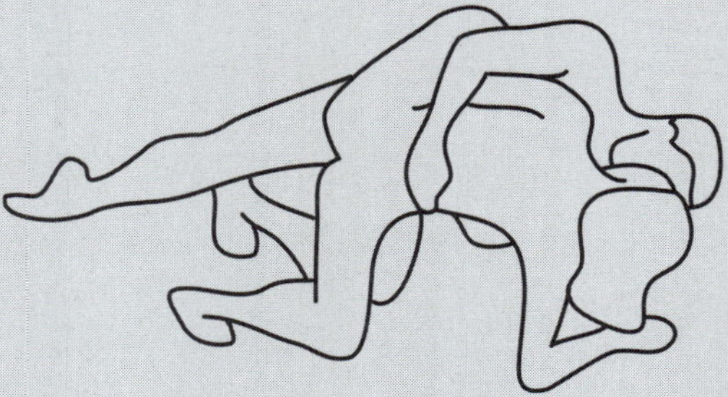

RIGHT FOOT RED

october.)

26

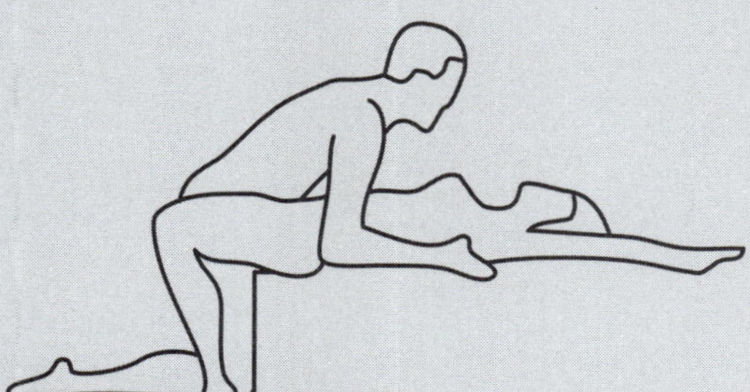

THE BODY SURF

october.) **27**

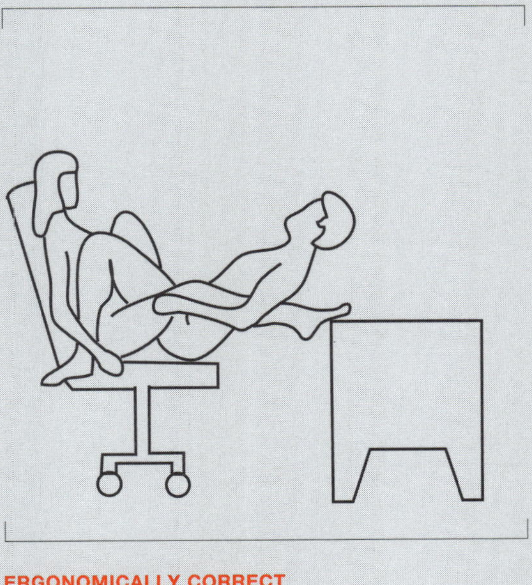

ERGONOMICALLY CORRECT

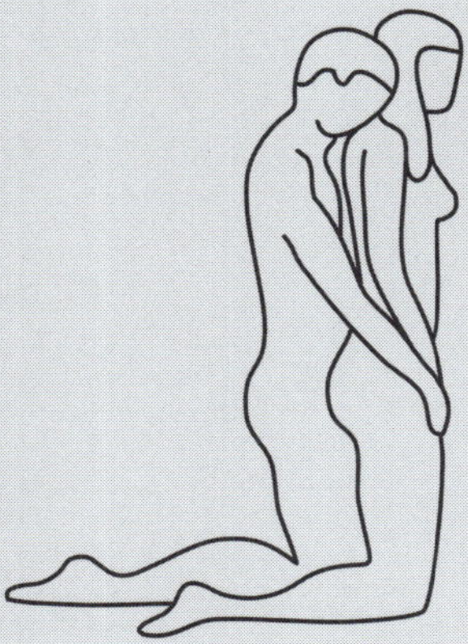

GETTIN' IT ON BENDED KNEE

october.) 29

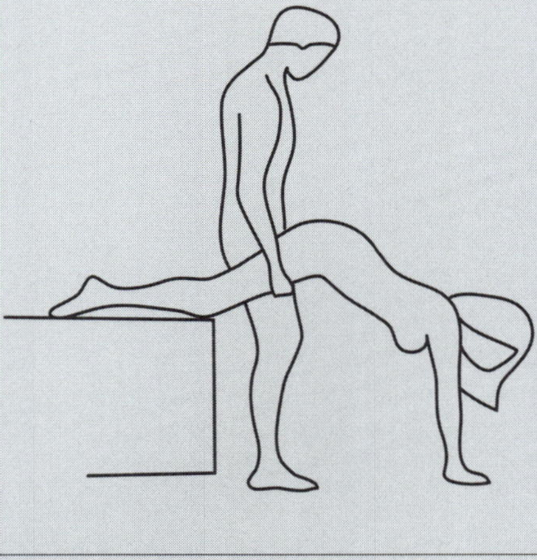

THE WARP AND WEFT

THE CLING WRAP

october.)

31

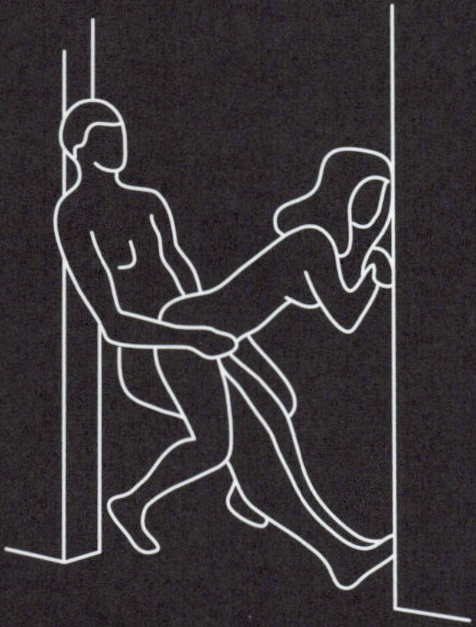

TRICK OR TREAT

november.) **01**

THE CUSHION PIN

november.) 02

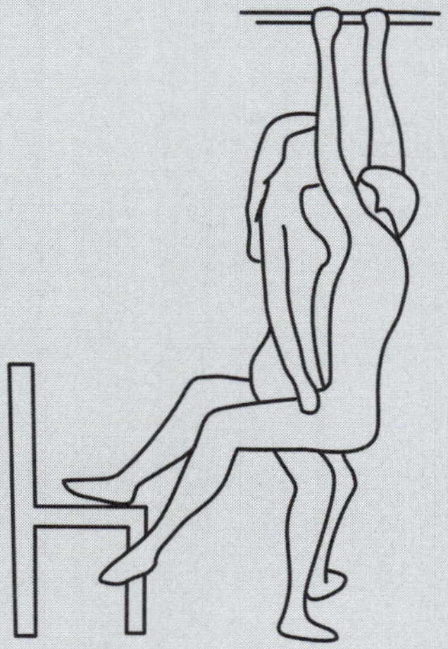

WELL HUNG

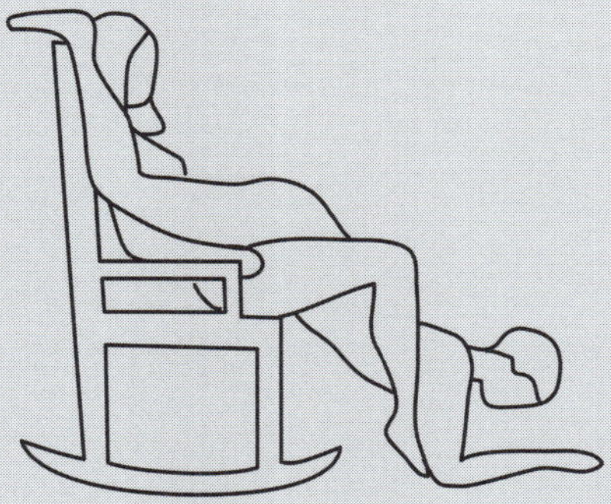

THE ENTWINEMENT

november.)

04

THE LOVER'S KNOT

05

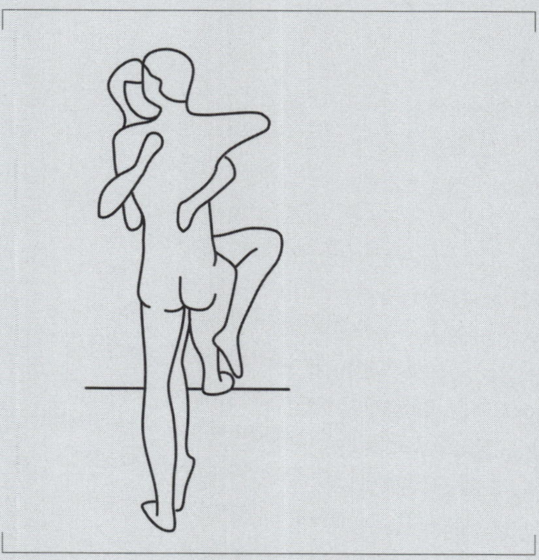

STAIRWAY TO HEAVEN

november.) **06**

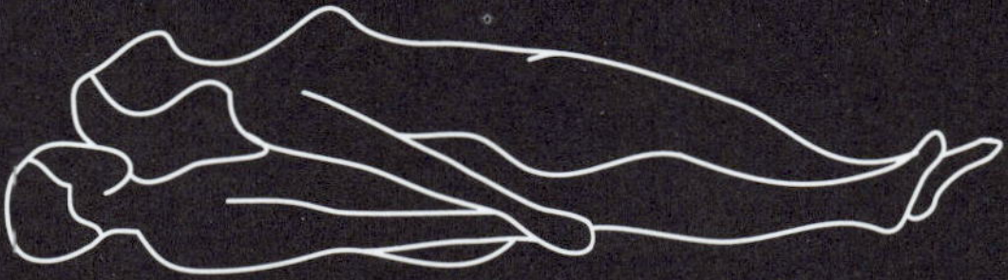

LIGHT AS A FEATHER . . .

november.) 07

THE WALL-MOUNT

november.)

08

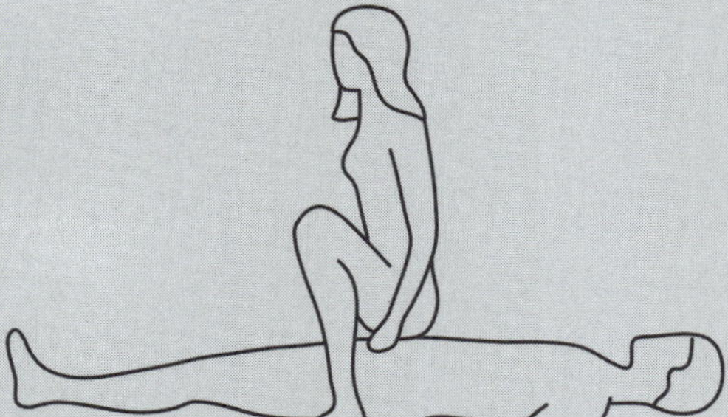

THE SWEDISH PUMP

november.) 09

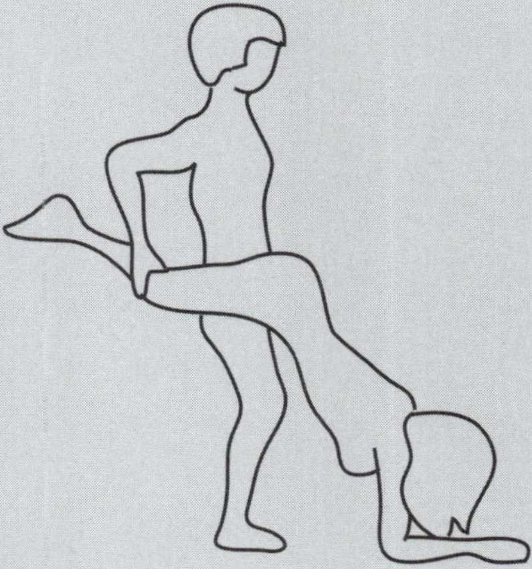

THE SNOW BLOWER

november.)

10

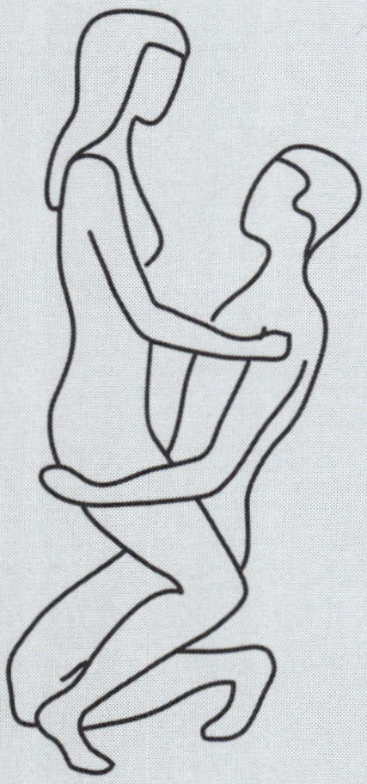

RIDING HIGH

THE CROTCH ROCKET

november.) **12**

THE LUGE

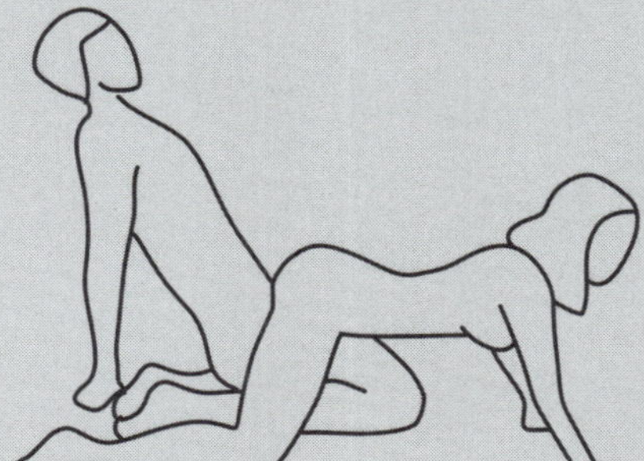

THE BOBSLED

november.) 14

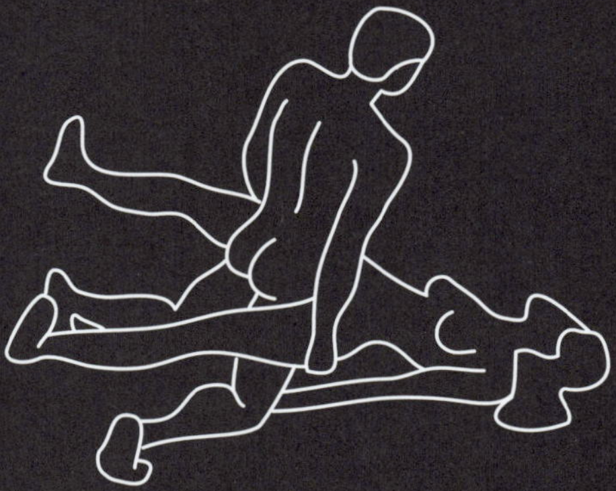

PULL MY LEGS

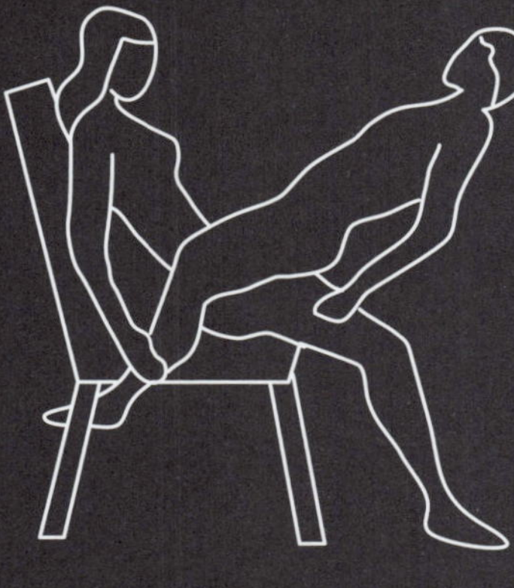

THE LIFT-OFF

november.) 16

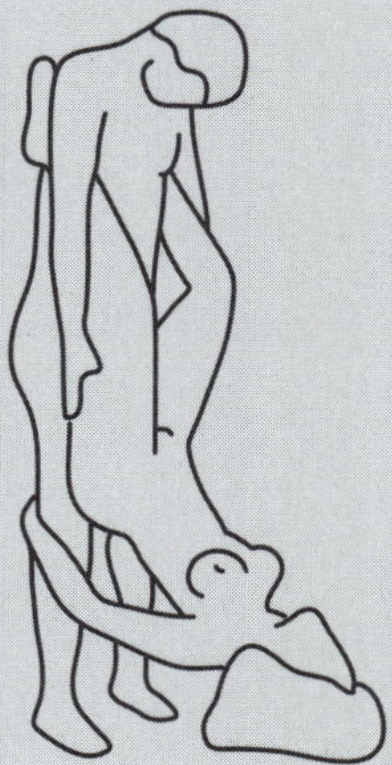

THE TOPSY-TURVY

november.)

17

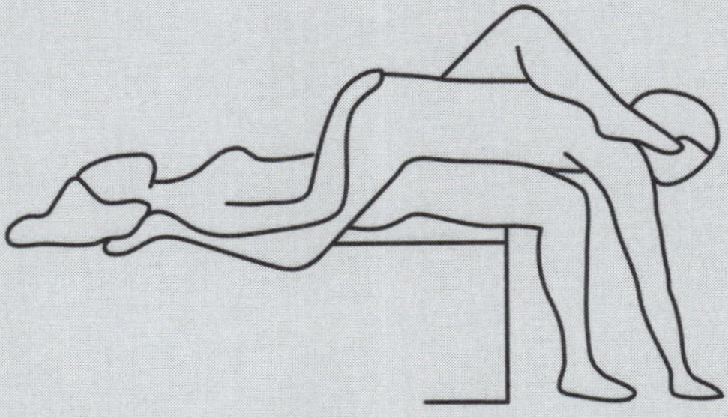

THE SLOW GETAWAY

ncvember.)

18

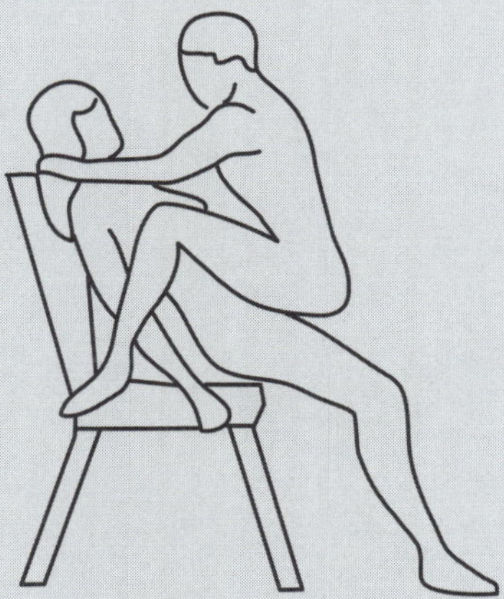

JOCKEYING FOR ATTENTION

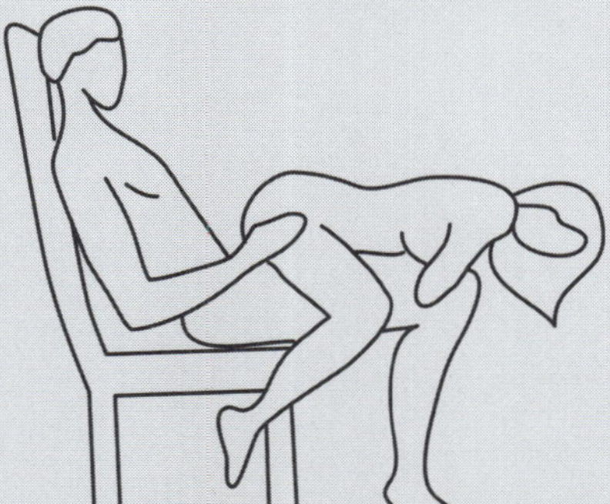

THE LAP JOINT

november.)

20

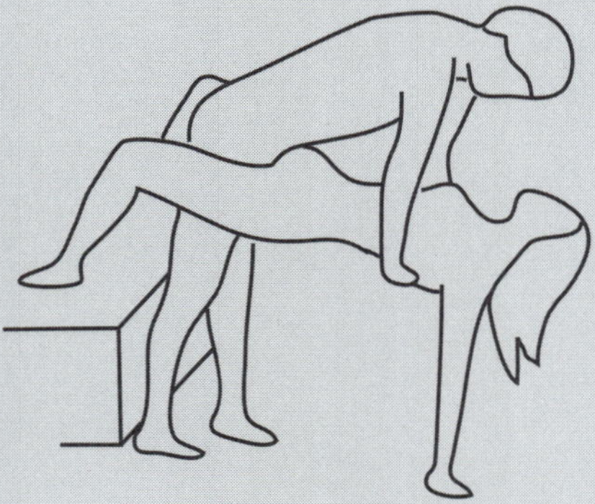

THE DIP STICK

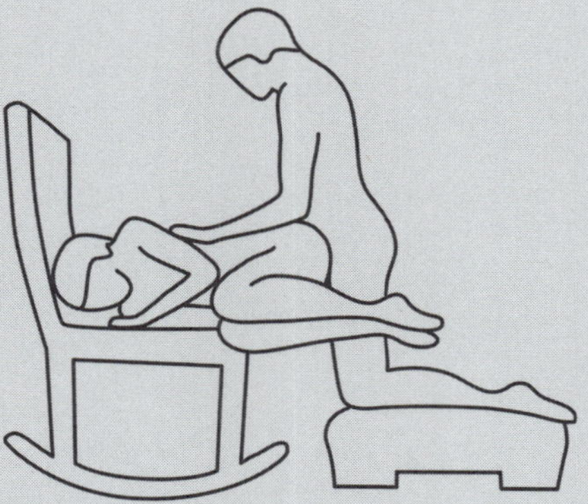

THE MASHED POTATO

november.)

22

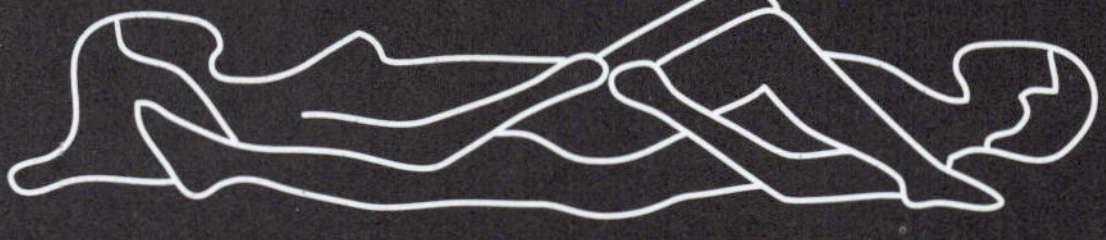

LOW-IMPACT AEROBICS

A NEW SLANT

november.) 24

THE EARTHQUAKE

november.)

25

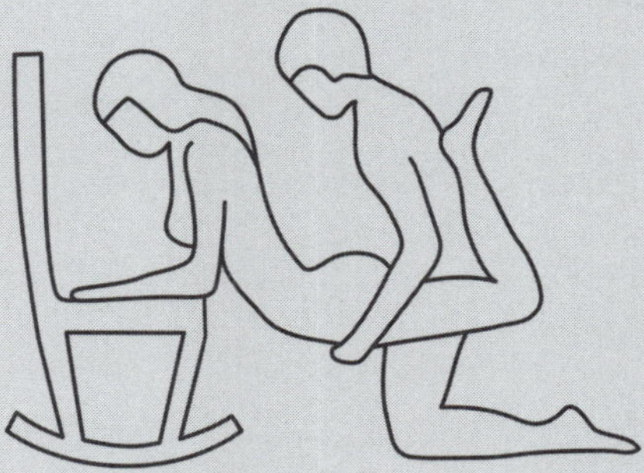

THE STEM TO STERN

november.) 26

THE ALPINE DOWNHILL

november.)

27

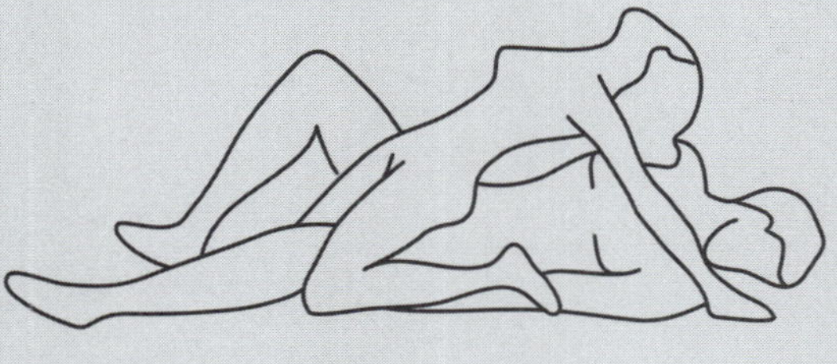

STARGAZING

november.) 28

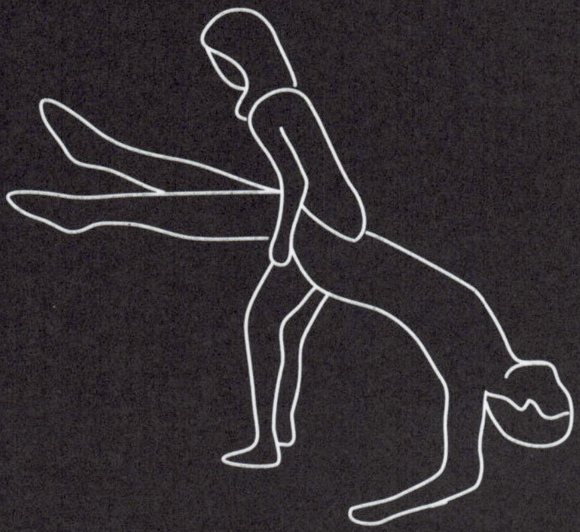

THE HOT AND HEAVY

THE STIFF NECKER

ncvember.) 30

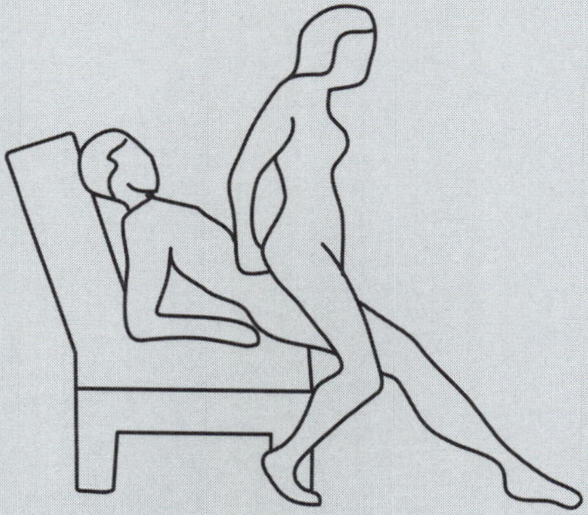

THE WATER SLIDE

december.)

01

THE NECK & NECK

december.) **02**

THE PROPOSAL

december.)

03

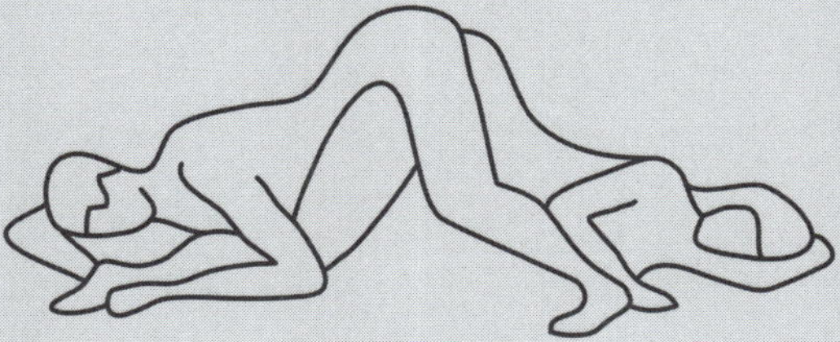

THE MODERN DANCERS

december.) **04**

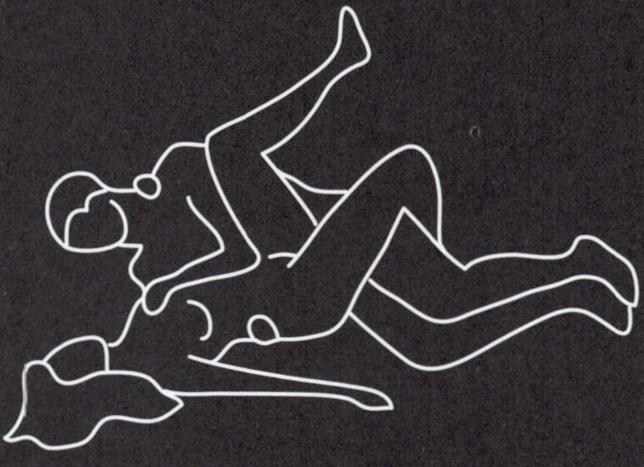

TAKING THE FALL

december.)

05

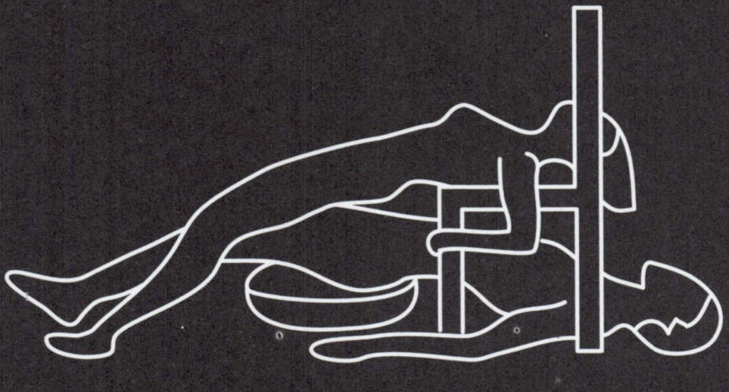

THE CHAIR LIFT

december.)

06

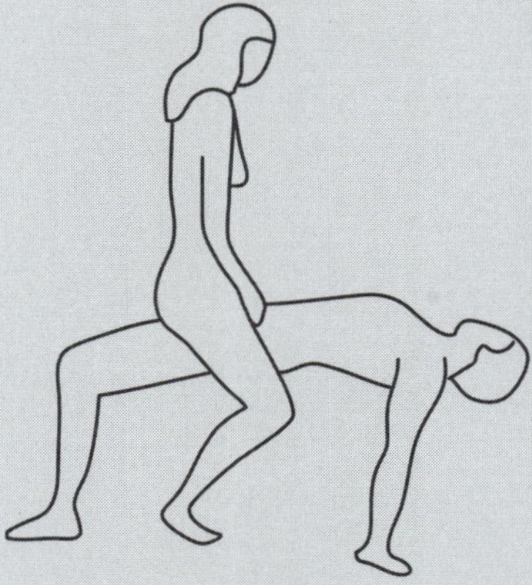

THE LADY GODIVA

december.) 07

RIDING SIDESADDLE

december.)

08

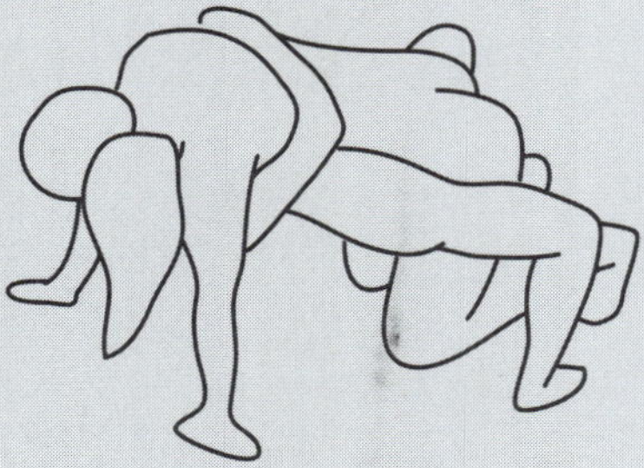

THE LOCKBOX

december.)

09

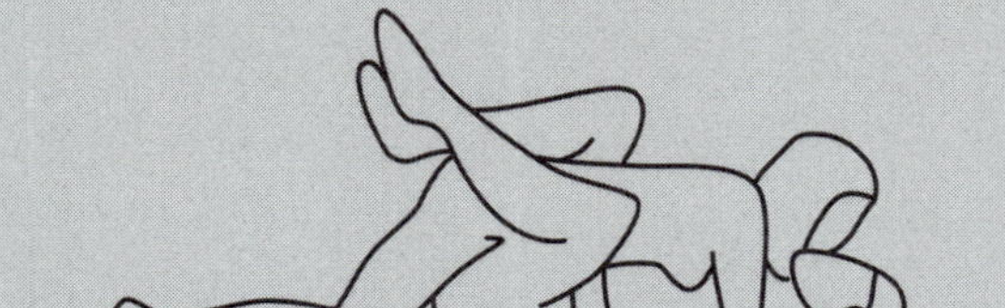

THE HOMECOMING

10

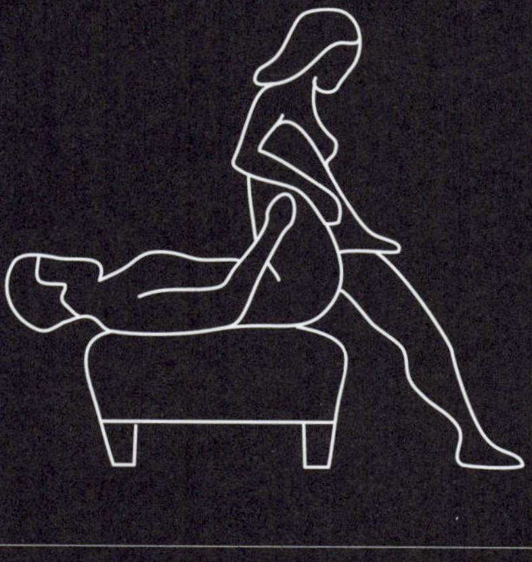

THE SKI LIFT

THE ROCKET LAUNCHER

december.)

12

LEG LIFTS

december.)

THE SERENDIPITOUS TRIP

december.) 14

THE THREE O'CLOCK

december.)

15

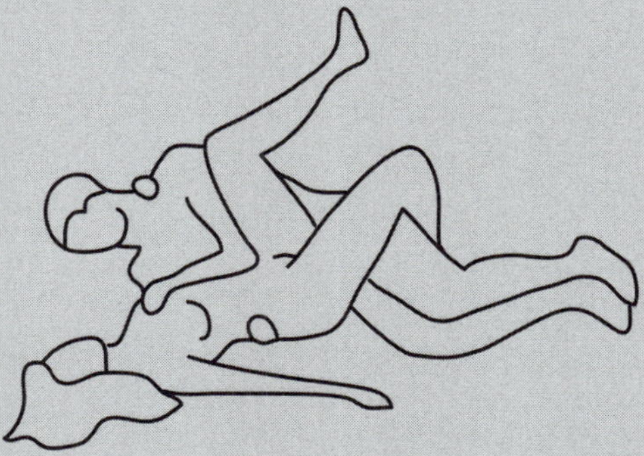

FALLING FOR YOU

december.) 16

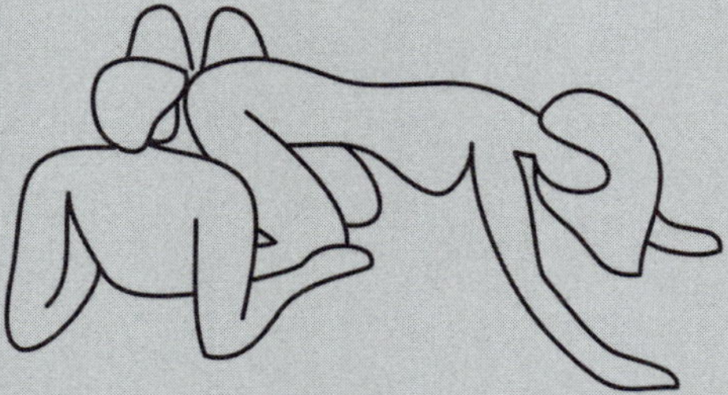

THE PUBE CRAWL

december.)

17

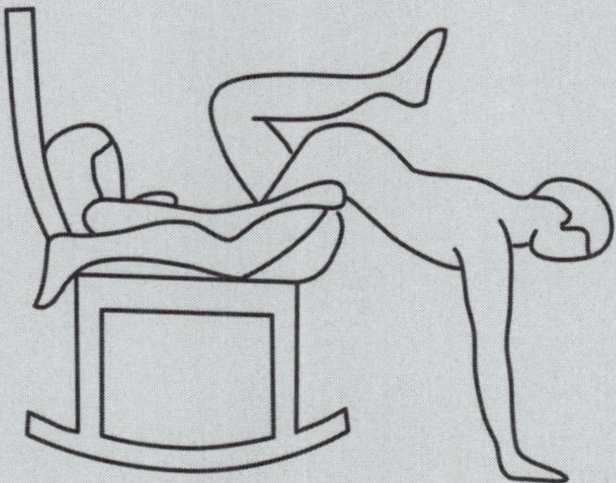

THE RAINY DAY

december.) 18

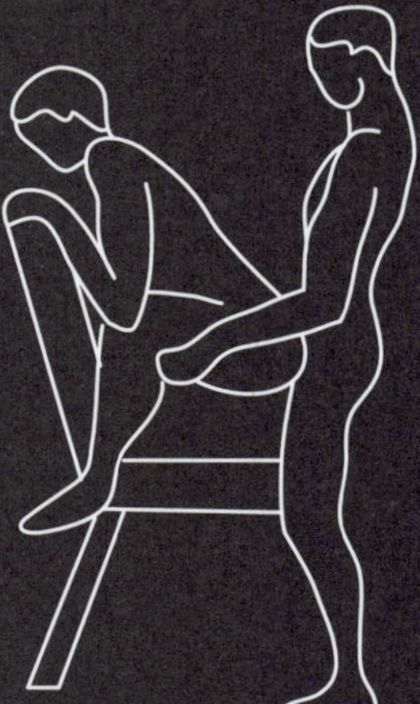

THE BODY LIFT

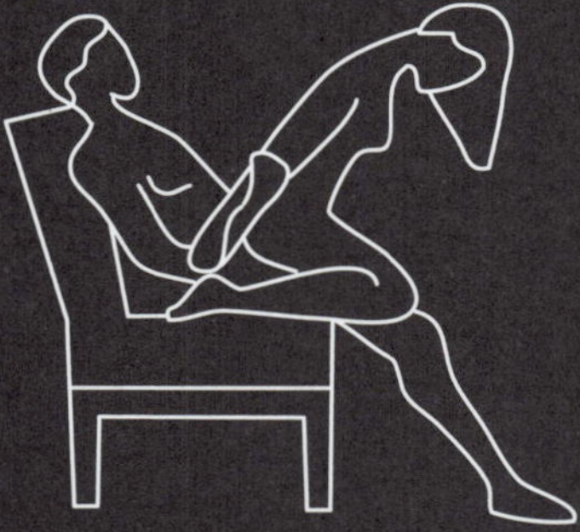

THE GET READY, GET SET

december.)

20

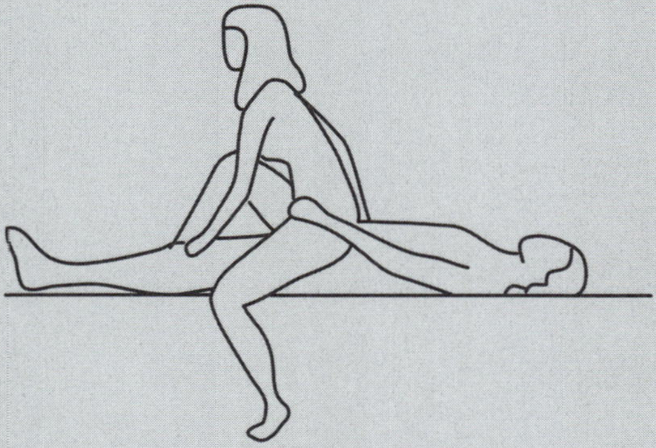

THE FENCE SITTER

december.)

21

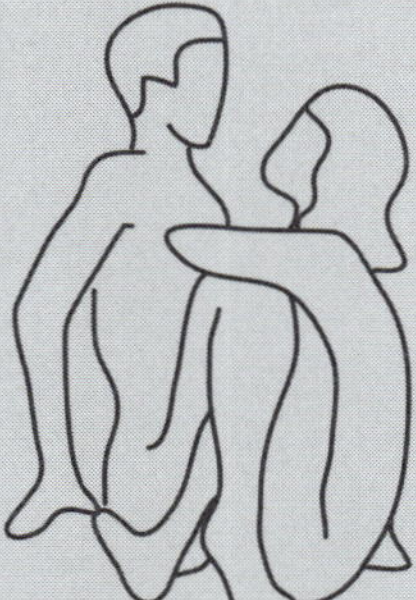

THE FOLDING CHAIR

december.) 22

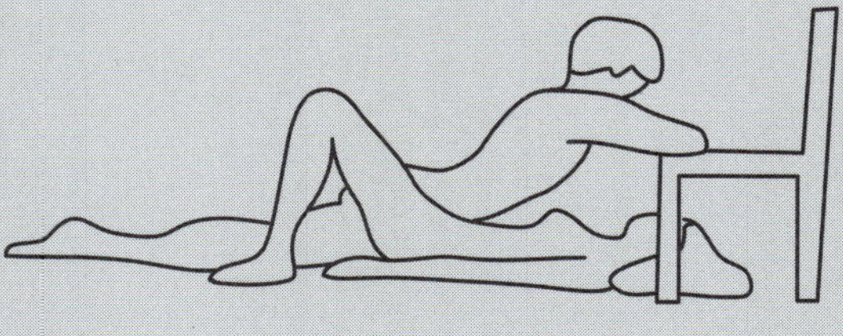

THE TAKE IT EASY

december.)

23

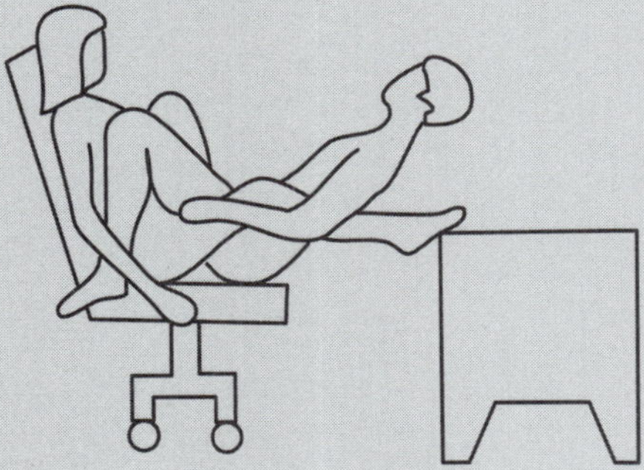

ON THE MOVE

december.)

24

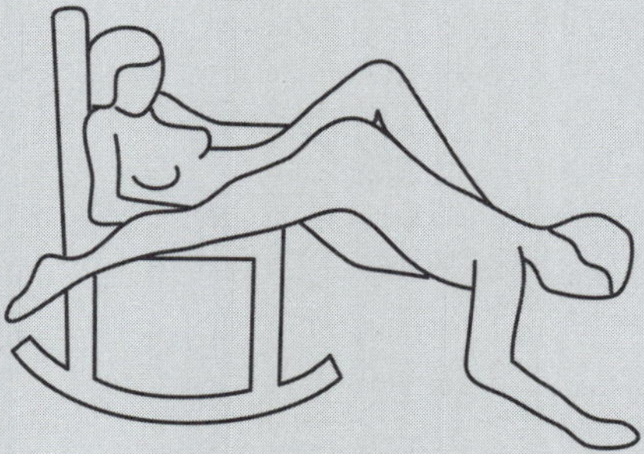

THE NUTCRACKER

THE BEST GIFT OF ALL

december.) 26

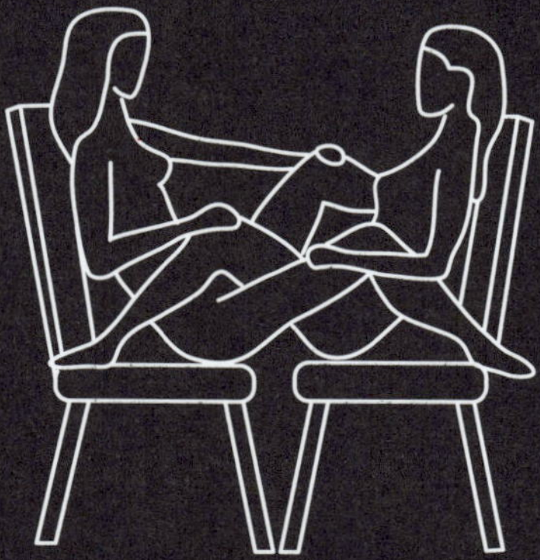

STACKING THE BOXES

THE SALTY PRETZEL

december.) 28

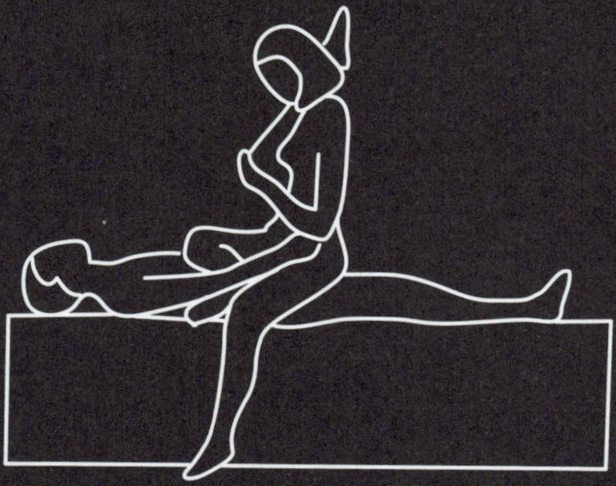

THE ACHILLES

THE PINWHEEL STICK

december.)

30

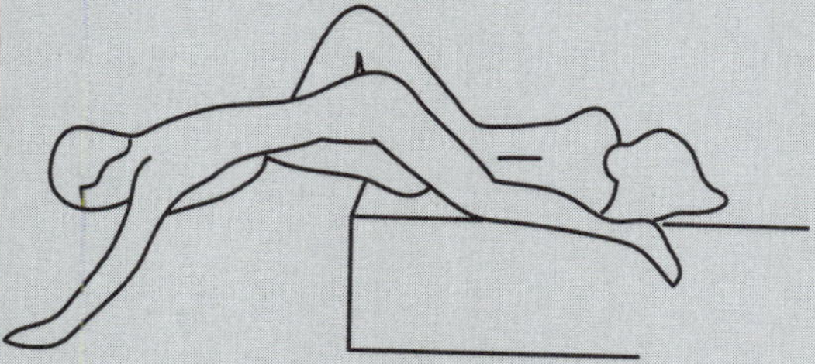

THE SCISSORS

december.)

31

THE END IS NEAR

BIO

>

Nerve.com was a popular online magazine about sex, relationships, and culture. Founded in 1997, *Nerve* published award-winning essays, provocative photography, and stimulating reporting for nearly two decades. Described by *Entertainment Weekly* as "*Playboy*'s body with *The New Yorker*'s brain," the website won numerous awards, including National Magazine Award nominations and Webby Awards.